OOPS!

OOPS!

An Insider's Guide To DATING, SEX, & RELATIONSHIPS In Your 20s

JULIE LAUREN

Any application of the recommended material in this book is at the sole risk of the reader, and at the reader's discretion. Responsibility of any injuries or other adverse effects resulting from the application of any of the information provided within this book is expressly disclaimed. Any resemblance to real persons, living or dead, is purely coincidental.

Published by Gatekeeper Press
3971 Hoover Rd. Suite 77
Columbus, OH 43123-2839

Cover Artwork by Merilliza Chan
Editing by Monica Wanat

ISBN (paperback): 9781619849501
eISBN: 9781619849495

Printed in the U.S.A

To learn more and connect with Julie,
visit www.byjulielauren.com.

You have recently graduated college and you have moved to Manhattan (or some other fabulous place.) Your dreams are awaiting. You're in the city that never sleeps, after all. You are meeting new people and hot on the dating scene. While I'm not a licensed therapist nor am I a doctor, I am a girl who has navigated NYC life, dated, hooked up, been heart broken, and had one hell of a time along the way. What you are holding in your hands is a handbook full of factual experiences and my observations. In the pages ahead, you will read about the harsh realities of men and women in their 20s when it comes to dating, relationships, and sex. I warn you; I can be blunt. It's real. It's raw. Think *Sex and the City* meets *He's Just Not That Into You*.

You're welcome.

Love always,

Julie

I dedicate this book to my friends who I have experienced some of my best moments with in New York City. Because of your stories, this handbook is possible. And now girls and guys in their 20s can not only enjoy our escapades, but learn something, as well. I love you, ladies.

Julie

TABLE OF CONTENTS

ACKNOWLEDGEMENTS

Oh, where to begin.

First, I want to thank you, the person who is about to read my first ever book. I truly hope you enjoy it.

A massive thank you goes out to my husband, my parents, and the rest of my family for always being nothing less than absolutely and incredibly supportive of me. Sometimes I have crazy dreams, but the fact that they always have my back means everything.

To my friends – you know who you are, thank you. Thank you for always supporting me and being there for me. I couldn't do it without you. And to the ones who helped with the title of my book and gave me their opinions whenever I asked. A special call out to my NYC girls – this book wouldn't have been possible without you and your stories. It was sure one hell of a time we had.

Mark Darren – thank you for contributing some of your amazing stories and words of wisdom. We always enjoyed comparing notes from both sides of the fence.

To Rob and the rest of the Gatekeeper Press team – thank you for making this dream of mine come to life.

A published book. Wow. It's hard to believe that something I have dreamt of since I was a little girl has finally happened. Don't ever give up on your dreams. No dream is too big. If you want it, go for it. Do it. Nothing is stopping you. Nothing at all.

THANK YOU!

Julie

Chapter 1

CONFUSION (and after reading the following you should not be in this state of mind anymore)

Looking back on my college years, I feel I was such a fool. I can admit it now, but back then, I truly made up every excuse under the sun for what it meant when I got the 2am text message from the boy I was swooning over. It took me a few years but then I finally realized what it didn't mean. It did NOT mean he liked me. In fact, it meant he had very little respect for me and strictly wanted to use me for a 'sexy time' situation. This leads me to…

No, a 2:30am text message does not mean he likes you

OK, ladies – let's break this down. As it's been pointed out time and time again, if a guy likes you, he will do anything in his power to take you out and see you. However, let me clear something up that may have not been cleared up before – if he is only texting you at night on the weekends, this does not mean he wants you.

You're probably thinking: *That's not true. He ALWAYS messages me first on the weekends. If he didn't like me, he wouldn't do that.*

Oh, sweet girl. You're probably a beautiful girl who could get a wonderful guy, but this one you're hung up on does not want you in the way you hope he would. He messages you first – great, but he's messaging you at 2am on a Friday. Earth to you, sweet girl, he's HORNY. He's a guy in his mid-20s who, yes, may find you quite attractive, but he doesn't want to date you. He doesn't want to hang out with you sober. He solely wants you for what you give him sexually. If you're OK with this, then by all means, have fun and enjoy this no strings attached situation, but I can promise you – this will not turn into a relationship, a marriage, and a white picket fence.

If you're a young 20 something girl and are having fun while not getting hurt, this isn't such a bad option. If you start having feelings for him though—and, be honest with yourself, because you are the one who will suffer—just stop.

If you can manage this sort of situation though, play away, my dear!

Just remember – when the clock starts ticking to the wee early hours of the morning and the texts start being exchanged, sex is sex, and it's strictly JUST sex when it's being propositioned at 2am.

Like I said, I'm going to be brutal with you, and please don't hate me for it.

You'll thank me one day, I pinky promise!

Something that used to come up a lot with my guy and girl friends would be the conversation about playing hard to get ('the game,' so to speak) and when it crosses the line. There are times when playing this 'game' is beneficial and effective, but there are times when it can drive a guy (or girl) almost mental!!

Playing Hard to Get vs. Not Interested

There has been enough talk to last us years explaining that it is very unlikely a boy is interested in a girl if he's not actively pursuing her and making a valiant effort to be with her. Well, what about the other way around?

Let me set the stage for you – you're out at a bar on the Lower East Side, you meet a girl through a friend of a college friend of a camp friend who knew this girl growing up. You know all the same people, go to all the same places, and you really hit it off. You talk for the rest of the night, buy her drinks, get her number, make a tentative plan for next week to take her out, play tonsil hockey for a bit, and the night is over. You go to bed feeling like, "Wow, I may have just met a girl I really could like." And we all know this isn't a common feeling among men in their mid-20s these days. It's not SO often you meet a girl you think you could really like beyond a hook up.

You debate messaging her the next day, but figure why not? You say you enjoyed meeting her and are looking forward to taking her out for drinks next week. She responds saying the same. All is grand.

On Monday, you call her, and she doesn't answer. Fine. Maybe she's playing hard to get. She texts you back an hour later saying she's still at work, going straight to dinner afterwards, but will try to call later.

You don't want to miss the opportunity so you say, "No problem, just wanted to figure out a day to take you out for drinks. How's Thursday?"

She responds, "Aw I don't know if I can – I have coworker plans. Sorry!"

This continues when trying to set up a date with her. Over that next weekend you message her to see what she's doing, she responds, and you meet her out at night a few drinks deep. Tonsil hockey takes place again and you even share a cab home this time. *OK, this is my chance*, you're thinking. *She's definitely interested.* However, she still plays the "not sure if I can this week" card, and you're stumped and confused.

What does this mean? You're probably a great looking guy and this rarely happens to you, but when it does you're so confused! Poor boy.

OK, my dear, let me tell you, being a girl and having been in this situation before -while I enjoyed hanging out with you when out at night, I enjoyed kissing you, but I just didn't see this going beyond that. Something just was not there. Maybe the girl just doesn't see herself dating you, maybe you're not her '"typical" type, maybe she thinks you're too nice, and she can't imagine you "throwing her down" and taking charge. There are a million reasons!

So, while it's easy to say a guy isn't into a girl if he's not making an effort, it's also easy to say a girl isn't into a guy when she's unresponsive. The "hard to get" banter can only happen for so long. If it continues beyond a couple weeks, and she's still NOT responsive to your attempts at a date, move on. Whatever you do, don't become annoying. Try a few times, and only for a couple weeks max, and then MOVE ON.

Many times, this girl will wonder where you went and why you stopped trying. This could work in your favor, and she'll realize while you may not be who she envisioned dating, she should give you a chance. I mean you pursued her for days on end – it's the least she can do. And if she doesn't wonder or care why you stopped trying, then who cares. She's not worth it, and move on to your next victim.

It's not hard. It shouldn't be complicated. If she's into you, you'll know.

Ladies, ladies, ladies – clinginess is NOT a good thing. Having your own life is! What a novel concept.

Stage 5 Clingers

Boys, this one is dedicated to you (but, girls, PLEASE read it because we really don't want a *Swimfan: The Sequel* coming to theaters based on your life.)

Here is a true story that I'm sure many of you have experienced in one form or another: You, as the guy, are super into this hot, confident (at the time, at least), sweet, funny, great girl. You talk a lot, mostly on a friendly level with some flirty banter thrown in. You want her even more because she makes you really try. She's a challenge. She still appears interested, but also a bit aloof (which you like.)

Let's fast forward.

A few weeks later (after a couple of dates you think go pretty well) you meet out at a bar on a Saturday night. You finally kiss. And you both feel something. SCORE. YES. The girl you've been gushing over is truly into you, as well.

Fast forward again.

A couple of sleepovers happen. Some good hook ups. Things are good. You REALLY like this girl. And she seems to REALLY like you, too.

Fast forward one more time.

You have sex. It's great sex. Well, the first time you were super nervous so Missy Elliott's "One Minute Man" is playing in your head, BUT the second time (that very same night) you make up for it and it is REALLY great sex. YES. SCORE AGAIN.

All of a sudden, this chick does a 180.

WHY?! WTF. WHY, WHY, WHY?!

You're pissed. You're pissed because she has become so f-ing annoying, but you REALLY liked her. *Why did she have to go crazy on me?!*

She texts ALL the time. She is in your face all day. She wants to hang out all the time. When you don't ask her out, she gets upset, makes you feel bad, and then she asks you out. There isn't a weekend night that goes by when she's not expecting to have a sleepover. On Sundays (your day of rest and relaxation) she's on your case. You are being driven semi-insane.

So, regardless of how much you really liked her, you can't handle it. This is NOT what you signed up for, so you end it.

...and another one bites the dust. Damn it.

OK, ladies – you have got to RELAX. Just because you have sex with this guy (who, yes, may be very much into you), it's still just sex until it becomes something more. If you can't handle having sex without getting attached, then hold off on it. Take a chill pill (literally). You need to EASE.

Guys hate more than anything a girl who is nudgy, needy, and annoying. The guy started to fall for you because you appeared confident, sure of yourself, and had a life outside of wanting him. And, yes, it's understood that you may become impatient or you may question if he is still into you, or you're scared because now you're starting to really like him and he's playing it cool.

You need to force yourself to stop thinking this way.

Calm down. Go do something. Go out with your friends. Go on other dates. Live your life. Don't wait around for him to ask you to do something. If he likes you, he'll ask you out. He really will. If he stops liking you for whatever reason, then move on. It wasn't meant to work out. NEXT.

Ladies, stop, take a look in the mirror, realize the worst thing you can do to guarantee ruining the potential of dating a guy, is to go from confident to crazy. This is never attractive, even on the prettiest of girls.

Some things are crystal clear with men, but some need to be explained because they cannot be fully understood easily, such as...

All talk, no action

This is something I used to not fully understand. I have to be honest – it was a bit confusing, and maybe some of you out there are currently feeling this way. I finally did understand, for example, if a guy didn't ask me out, he wasn't interested. If they only reached out to me at 2am on Fridays, they only wanted sex. I understood that.

What I didn't get was why guys would ask for a girl's number, but never actually use it. Various people have asked me this question many times before. *We literally hung out the entire night, he got my number, and it's been two weeks and nothing. Why did he even bother asking for it?!*

I, personally, feel if you, as the guy, know you will not be calling this girl ever, do not even bother getting her number. Really – there's no point. It's a waste of her time and yours to do the whole song and dance surrounding the getting of the number.

Guy: So, am I going to see you again?

Girl: I don't know, you tell me.

Guy: Can I get your number?

Girl: Of course! Want me to put it in? (Girl enters it because she is worried he won't hear her number over the loud music, and then enter the wrong number, and then never be able to reach her.) OH THE HORROR! (Please note the sarcasm.)

Guy: Awesome – I'll call you. Have a good night

NOT NECESSARY.

I truly feel just don't get the digits if you know you won't be using them. Girls would rather know off the bat that you're not that into them and that you're not actually going to follow through and call.

I asked a friend of mine, who also used to be the biggest ladies' man in Manhattan in his hay day for his opinion on the matter.

Ladies, listen up.

When a guy meets a girl out he is attracted to, he obviously would want to hook up with that girl on the spot. It is due to "the game' that he realizes that he needs to get the girls number so that he can follow up at another time, go on a date, meet up, and so forth, and hopefully close the deal.

There are rare occasions where the girl will actually go home with the guy on the night he meets her, but guys do not typically count on that happening. Guys are used to asking a girl for her number out of routine. We do it because we plan on meeting up with that girl again and trying to hook up with her obviously. We sometimes get multiple girls' numbers in a night. (Let's face it – girls give out their numbers a lot, too.)

Something happens the next day (or couple days later) though when a guy decides what to do with that girl's number… He is SOBER! He is not thinking the exact same way he was when he met her. He goes and tries to stalk her on Facebook. (You do it too girls-don't deny it!) He wants to remember what she looks like. He also asks his friends about her to find out their opinions. After all this research and taking into account his current dating situation (i.e., other "projects" he is working on), he will decide whether to follow up with the girl (text, call, etc.) to try and make plans.

At this point, if a guy does not deem it worth following up (girl not hot enough, too many mutual friends, etc.), girls should be thankful that he is not wasting your time. After all, girls do the same to guys in reverse by not answering and blowing us off if not interested.

The lack of deal closing once numbers are exchanged can be mostly blamed on the following: most of the time, the guy and/or girl is drunk and would have hooked up with the other person that night if they had tried; however, nothing happened because both parties were following the rules of "the game."

And there you have it. I guess it all makes sense now!?

Moral of the story: when you're meeting out, far from sober, everything is a bit hazy. Why do you think there is the phrase "beer goggles"? Once sober and in the daylight, it's a whole different ballgame, and at this point it is when the boy will reassess the situation.

So, ladies, when you're out this weekend – do not be surprised or get mad if some hot stallion gets your number and doesn't use it. In fact, try to forget (and depending on how much you drink, it may be quite easy to forget) you even gave your number out. That way, if this person ends up calling you, it'll be a pleasant surprise.

Are we all clear now?

Playing games is sometimes fun and sometimes quite necessary. There comes a point, though, when it gets to be too much, when it just doesn't help the situation anymore.

Playing "hard to get" – when is it enough?

I know of the following situation (and you likely have been IN the following situation, girls): there is a boy you are seemingly interested in and the feelings seem to be mutual. You are showing interest and he's reciprocating. All of a sudden, you realize you may not be feeling it anymore or you get distracted with another boy. The original guy is now IN YOUR FACE. He tries to make plans, calls a lot, and pursues you in a BIG way. He's visibly all of a sudden crazy about you. A couple months later, you realize you may want to pursue him again (or attempt it) because you know deep down he's such a good guy and worth a shot (especially after how much he chased you.) You show interest again, and now he's back to playing the aloof card.

Now you're confused. *I understand the concept of "playing hard to get," but isn't it enough now?!*

I conversed with my guy pal on this one because, I have to be honest; this is something I don't fully understand. I understand a "challenge" is much more appealing and fun for a guy, but if the feelings are there, is there really a need for the back and forth: aloof, interested, aloof, interested? I mean it seems a bit exhausting if you ask me.

I will tell you that after I discussed the following with him, I was a tiny bit upset at the time (because I had recently been in a similar situation.) I said, "I don't like your harshness at the moment. Are you sure this is accurate?!"

He said, "Yes, I've been in the situation before. It really is how guys feel. Our pride gets hurt after we chase a girl for a while with no success."

FINE.

Here goes.

"Basically, guys like the chase (to an extent.) However, they genuinely get fed up and turned off by a girl who is not interested. If a girl plays games, they still will think she is hot and obviously would still hook up with her. (Few guys let their principles get in the way of getting laid.) But... they will NOT be as into her anymore.

Playing hard to get gets old after a while, and the other person starts to think you simply don't want them. No girl wants to feel unwanted, so what makes it OK to act that way towards a guy?

Indifference is not nice either, ladies. If you are not into it, save them the headache and time and ignore them or better yet, TELL THEM! Don't worry, they are big boys and will shake it off and find somebody better who will actually give them the time of day.

Now, for you girls who think you are entitled to go after a guy weeks, months, or even years later, after you have made him feel bad by not acting interested, YOU HAVE GOT TO BE KIDDING!

Any guy that gives into you for more than the sex he is owed for his previous efforts is not a man at all. If you were not interested the first time around, you obviously were just not into that person. The only justifiable reason for acting uninterested during round one would be if you were dating somebody at the time without the other person knowing. (Shady, shady.)

Guys need to be smart and see that you are only reaching out to them because you are clearly not getting enough action lately, you're bored, and are fishing through your phone and Facebook for any guy that will hook up, literally. They should get the sex they deserve for being made to feel insignificant—yes ladies, men have feelings too—but under no circumstances should they be foolish and show you feelings or like you again. After all, there is an extremely high likelihood that you will just dump them like a bad habit once you find somebody else you are really into anyways.

I, as the girl, am chiming in here – I strongly *believe there are exceptions, but we can get to those later on.*

In conclusion, do the guys a favor: if you don't act interested in them during round one, don't reach out to them later. Stick it out a little bit longer until you find a guy you actually are interested in!

You have a boyfriend or girlfriend – you should be proud of your significant other. You shouldn't try to hide it when you're out. I get it, sometimes it's fun to flirt "harmlessly." That's only fine to do when the other person isn't swooning over you. Make sure not to lead the person on ALL night for crying out loud.

Hi, my name is Taken – it's nice to meet you

I was out for drinks one night in the city way back with some girl friends. No agenda in mind – just in the mood for some adult beverages and harmless Tuesday night fun. Easy enough, right?

We show up at one of our favorite bars, sit at a table, are gabbing away, and some attractive men —yes, I say "men"" because they were in their upper 20s – and by this point, I like to assume they are "men", contrary to popular belief —sit at the table and join us. *How presumptuous of them to assume we wanted them to sit with us on girls' night!* They were cute, though, so we didn't stop them.

There happened to be 3 of them – 3 of us…well, that works well. (No, we didn't have a gang bang – don't get too excited, dear readers.) The one who started talking to me was tall, dark, and handsome. *OK, fine, I won't make up an excuse to get you to leave. At the very least, you're enjoyable eye candy.* An hour later I realize this guy is actually pretty funny and seemingly very cool. A couple hours later, my friends and I decide to go. Mr. Tall Dark and Handsome asks for my number, and as we were saying goodbye he goes (and I quote) "I just want to tell you – I actually have a girlfriend. Granted, it's only been a few months, but a girlfriend, nonetheless. I think you're really cool, though, and I'd love to hang out, as friends, sometime. Hope that's cool."

HUH?

Now, I'm all about guy friends. There's nothing wrong with that, and in fact, I love and cherish my guy friends. They are so much fun and are great sounding boards. They have knocked sense into my head and they are great to talk to (and they can be really blunt, too, which is sometimes necessary.) HOWEVER, after three hours of talking to someone (and, yes, flirting was involved), it didn't seem this was going in the "Hey, let's be friends" direction. Not that it was going in any direction necessarily, but the last thing I thought was that he had a girlfriend!

I really wasn't THAT upset. I quickly got over it, but it just confused me. Why didn't he mention this sooner? I don't need him to wear a t-shirt that says, "I have a girlfriend at the moment, but I still like to hit on girls." I didn't need him to say, "Hi I'm (insert name here), and I have a girlfriend. What's your name?"

I didn't need him to even bring her up within the first 10 minutes. I just figured, at one point during the three hours we were talking, he would throw the word "girlfriend" into one of his sentences. Nope.

I think it's perfectly fine if men with girlfriends still go out with their friends, have fun, even talk to girls. (In fact, they should.) I just wouldn't like my guy to actively hit on a girl and get her number. There is a difference between talking to a girl while being friendly and actually hitting on a girl while flirting. And, yes, I know the difference. I've met enough men in my day. This guy was not JUST being friendly.

Was he in a fight with his girlfriend at the moment? Was he getting bored with her? Was he questioning things? Was he actually looking to cheat on her? Was he doubting their relationship and how she feels about him? Who knows!

And what was he going to do with my number exactly? Call me up, ask me for a drink while the girlfriend was at spinning class, and then eventually ask me to jump in on a threesome? (Ok, maybe that was his plan.) I mean – I don't think said girlfriend would be happy with this. And, yes, I did get a text later that evening: "Great to meet you – we should get together soon." Hmmmm.

Now, those of you boys with girlfriends out there – I'm not saying you can't look at other women or talk to other women even. You really should continue doing both (in a harmless way, of course). I'm just saying if you're playing "wingman" at a bar one night or if you're just up for being friendly, somehow throw it into conversation that you are not single. For example, if you're talking about restaurants, throw in, "*Yeah, I took my girlfriend there last week.*"

Or if you're talking about where you're from and she happens to say Westchester, and your girlfriend happens to be from there – "*Oh, my girlfriend is from there, too.*"

Or if you're talking about upcoming weekend plans, say, "*I think my girlfriend and I are going to do x, y, or z on Saturday.*" Or if you're talking about where you went to school and it's where your girlfriend went, then note, "*My girlfriend went there.*" There are ways to do this appropriately!

If the girl you're talking to happens to be attracted to you or even thinks she may end up in your bed later that night, she should know sooner rather than later that you are off limits in that department. I know you may enjoy talking to her, but she should still be aware. Some girls will peace out from the conversation as soon as they hear "girlfriend," but some will continue talking.

I will also say that unless you are getting the number of this girl to give to your single friend you think he'd like, there is no need to get her number. I mean, are you really looking for friends who happen to be girls at this age, while having a girlfriend? Likely not. There is nothing wrong with having female friends. In fact, I encourage it, but unless you are 100% not sexually attracted to said girl at bar, are you really looking to be her "friend" while you are with your girlfriend? Again, likely not. But hey – on the off chance you are – make sure she knows this will JUST be a friendship.

And, ladies, you're not getting off the hook so easily here. All of this applies to you, as well. I know it happens more often than not a guy will be hitting on you, you have a boyfriend, and you happen to leave that one fact out about yourself. Finally, you tell the guy as he's leaving the bar (after he gets your number and talks to you for hours) or you let him take your number, even "sext" you, and you finally throw it out there that, hey, you're not single. At all.

As I said – same applies! Somehow you've got to throw it in there that you have a boyfriend. Maybe not right away, but at some point during the conversation, it should be known. I know from too many of my guy friends that it couldn't be more annoying to talk to a girl all night and finally when he goes to get the digits she says "Oh, sorry – I actually have a boyfriend, but great to meet you!" *Ugh, waste of time.*

Now, some boys don't mind this because they just enjoyed the conversation all night (and they will try to pursue you regardless of the fact that you are not available). Most guys, however, this bothers. They either wanted to attempt taking you home that night or they wanted to ask you on a date soon after. Well, that just got shot to shit.

I get it – sometimes it's just fun to harmlessly flirt with other men, but don't let it go too far. You wouldn't like it if your boyfriend was getting girls' numbers and flirting with other women, so don't do it to him.

In summary, if you're out at a bar without your significant other, somehow make it known at some point during your three hour banter back and forth with mystery person that you are not available. It's only fair.

Now, if you have an agreement with your boyfriend or girlfriend that you are trying to spruce things up in the department called your "sex life" and are looking to have a threesome, then that's another story and more power to you! If that's the reason you're getting this person's number, or giving your number, then that's another exception. Just make sure they know they are being propositioned for said activity.

OK, cool?

Glad we settled that one.

Is age just a number? Is going years above or below a good idea? Something worth trying? I'm all about it! If nothing else, it's great experience. And who wants to turn down THAT?!

How old is too old?

It's interesting – years back in my early to mid-20s I was "scared" of the 30 something guy. Seemed way too old for me. I thought they were all in another place – wanting marriage, kids, and a white picket fence, all very scary thoughts to me at that moment in time! I was still making decisions that I sometimes questioned the next morning. However, as my time in NYC went on, many of my dates were with those 30 something guys I used to be scared of! Oh the irony.

Ladies, they aren't so bad. Some of them are actually less ready for THAT (above) than the 20 something guys.

Case in point: my friend set me up with a man boy. (That's what I call them because by no means do they fall into the "men" category, but they are also very far from being a "boy" so they are MANBOYS.) He was very good looking, successful, great on paper, so I figured I'd give it a shot. He was going to be 33. That meant he was born in a different decade than I was! This made me think *OK he HAS to be on the wife hunt.* OY. Not what I was going for on that lovely Wednesday evening.

Lo and behold, we had a very fun date! Not someone I wanted to have a serious relationship with, but it was a fun night.

Turns out, he couldn't have been further from looking for a wife. Based on our conversations, it seemed he didn't "do" the girlfriend thing, and he was really just looking to have fun. At almost 33, I would assume he would want a relationship, but hey – more power to this guy. He was CERTAINLY living it up.

When I was in my early 20s, I had very close guy friends who were in their mid-20s and would have liked to wife it up right away – honest. Age truly has no bearing on these thoughts apparently!

Of course, there are your 20 something guys that want to sleep with a different girl each weekend and there are your 30 something guys who do want to meet wife material immediately if not sooner, BUT there are tons of outliers.

This is me telling you, ladies, do NOT say, "No," to a date because he is older or you are turned off by his age. It really means NOTHING. This I promise you. It makes it so much more exciting – being open to the 30 something manboys who can introduce you to a whole new world of guys.

As long as they haven't been married before (or aren't currently married) and they have no kids, you are good to go.

Here's to older men!

When I was dating, I was such a fan of the ever-so-famous book "He's Just Not That Into You." And this next topic may feel very similar to that, but I still feel it's necessary to cover, as it is a VERY popular topic. And it just comes down to men not being THAT hard to figure out after all.

Men aren't THAT hard to figure out

I hate to break it to you, but if you haven't heard from him in almost two weeks, he's not calling you.

Let's set the stage.

You're out at a bar, you meet some gorgeous guy (props to you), you hit it off, he buys you drinks, he gets your number, you have a little makeout sesh, you don't go home with him (impressive), and he says he wants to take you out and that he will call to follow up.

Wow. Sounds like a fabulous night. Good work, my friend!

Not so fast.

A few days go by and nothing, not even a text – fine, no big deal. Don't write him off yet.

A few more days go by and still nothing – write him off any day now.

Almost two weeks go by and NOTHING – done, done, DONE.

No, really, I mean this – he's NOT calling you. And if he does, he likely doesn't want anything more than a fun session in the sack.

Why?

If this guy were interested in you—beyond the initial drunk attraction at a bar at 11pm on a Saturday—he would have texted or called almost immediately. I know a lot of people don't fully believe in the book *He's Just Not That Into You*, but I have to say on many occasions that book is dead-on accurate.

Guys aren't that hard to figure out. Really – they're not! We make them out to be the most complex creatures, but they are really very transparent. You just have to know how to read them.

If a guy is into you, and I mean REALLY into you (beyond random sex), he will REALLY go above and beyond to take you out. If you meet him on Saturday night, he'll likely text (hopefully call, but not giving the boys SO much credit when it comes to that) the next day or the day after (sometimes that very night.) He'll want to set up plans that very next week. He doesn't want to wait around, play all these games, and ask you out in two weeks. He just doesn't.

A friend of mine met a really "great" guy way back. I mean he seemed really great, I have to say. They totally hit it off, spent the ENTIRE night talking, then playing tonsil hockey, and then he walked her home. (He didn't go up – she was trying to play this right). She could not have been more certain that he was going to follow through.

Three weeks later we're out, and she told me she hasn't heard a peep from him.

It seems mind boggling, but at the end of the day it comes down to—sorry to be harsh—he really just doesn't like you. He may have seemed interested four beers deep, in the mood of a dimly lit bar. But when day breaks, he's over it. Why? Don't know. Don't personally care.

Under no circumstances should you (directed towards the females reading) reach out to him. Why would you?!?!!?! If he wanted you, he would have contacted you. You contacting him is just silly. It makes you look dumb (and somewhat desperate.) You met out at night (not sober) – this is likely not your prince in shining armor. There will be another, I promise!

If you call him and he agrees to make a plan or ask you out, you'll never know if he REALLY wanted to go out with you to begin with because he didn't initiate it. Why would you want that?

Don't you want someone who WANTS you very badly? Like can't live without you badly?

Yes, that's what I thought.

So, next time you're out, and you meet some hot guy, and he doesn't call – please, for all our sakes, just move on. Like immediately.

I mean, if he does reach out weeks later to hang late night – just know what you're getting yourself into. I'll make it clear – you will be getting yourself into strictly a sexy time situation. Not necessarily a bad thing, but we need to make sure you're clear. THIS WILL BE FOR SEX. AND JUST SEX.

OHHHH, men.

Chapter 2

THE INTERNET. THE ROOT OF ALL EVIL?

We all love it. Some of us hate to admit it, but we all LOVE Facebook and Twitter and Instagram. Some of us could sit on these sites for HOURS "stalking"—oh man, that doesn't sound good – let's say perusing—our friends, frenemies, crushes, and ex-lovers' pictures, wall posts, and everything in between. I know people who honestly could turn their full-time job into this very thing. Hello, my name is (insert name here) and I work as a full time Facebook Peruser. Drinks this week? I wouldn't say it's something to be proud of, but it's certainly very relevant these days. All that being said, so many BAD things come from these amazing sites. I've dated guys where we've both mutually agreed to NOT become Facebook friends. It can be better off that way! However, Facebook isn't all bad; it's actually quite beneficial when the clock strikes 2am…

Facebook is the new booty call

This happened to me in NYC way back when.

It's 2:30am, my Blackberry vibrates. (It was back in the Blackberry days. Like I said, I'm "old.") It alerts me to a new Facebook notification. I have a message. "I know this is a random question, but what are you up to?" Of course it's a random question, silly boy. We haven't spoken in over a month, I never even saved your phone number, and you have the nerve to message me (not even via text) at 2:30 in the morning to ask what I'm doing? I'm insulted. Who do you think I am?!

Of course, the very next morning I immediately told my close guy friend, and I expressed how I was very offended that this boy had the balls to do such a thing!

"I've done that before," he says, 'but actually girls tend to do it to me a lot, too, strictly because they're horny." OK, so apparently I'm the one who needed to lighten up. Apparently sending a Facebook booty call is pretty common. Apparently it's a very clear way of saying "I couldn't be less interested in you, but it's late at night, I need some loving. You're easy. Let's do this."

I, personally, feel even a text would have sufficed enough. But a Facebook message? How impersonal can one get?!

While my guy friend thought it was quite the "thing" to do, I mean, hey, when you're far from sober and are looking for some late night action, and can't recall exactly what the girl (or guy) looks like who you met last weekend, why not do a little Facebook stalking followed by a Facebook booty call? I tended to feel otherwise.

So, ladies and gents, don't be alarmed if you receive a Facebook message late at night seeing what you're up to. It will not be because this person wants to catch up and talk – it will strictly be for sexy time.

11:00pm: breakup, 11:02pm: relationship status on Facebook changed to "single" – seriously?

This used to be one of my biggest pet peeves. The first thing you do after getting out of a serious relationship is run to Facebook to make sure the world knows you are single again? REALLY?

You've been dating your significant other for about a year and a half. The relationship had its ups and downs, but 90% of the time you were very much "in love." One thing leads to another and the spark just isn't there anymore. It's a mutual feeling, but by no means is it easy for either of you. You have an hour long conversation to try to figure it out, but ultimately decide to part ways. You both say your "final goodbye" and within 5 minutes you're not calling your friends to vent, scream, and cry, you're not cracking open a bottle of wine to drown your sorrows, you're not going on a run to clear your head; YOU ARE ON FACEBOOK CHANGING YOUR RELATIONSHIP STATUS.

Please tell me I'm not the only one who thinks this is slightly absurd.

I just don't get how after this serious relationship and the hard break up, it all comes down to a Facebook relationship status. Did it mean nothing more to you than that? Can you give yourself at the least a few days to be upset and then MAYBE think about Facebook? Don't get me wrong – it's not about not enjoying Facebook, but SERIOUSLY?

I'm truly sorry if I'm offending you, dear readers, by saying this (because I'm sure the majority of you have done this very thing), but I really just don't get it. No need to beat yourself up over it, though – now you know what not to do going forward!

And onto the next topic relating to Facebook and Social Media post break up: PHOTOS.

Yes, probably 97% of your photos are either you and your significant other (well, ex significant other) together or the two of you together with all your friends (people that became friends due to the two of you dating, and now it's going to be awkward because you can't all hang out again – but don't worry. I'll get to this later.)

So, you are questioning – do I remove every photo I posted of us? Do I detag myself from every picture I'm in with him/her, and do I act like this person never existed in my life? NO!

While I do agree, on some level, there is no need for 150

pictures of you and your ex all over Facebook, I don't think one needs to take such extreme measures as to delete and de-tag every single one.

Are you ashamed of what your ex looks like and don't want your future significant other to see him or her? (Well, that's just unfortunate and you probably should have thought about that PRIOR to dating them.) Are you so hurt by the breakup that it's just easier if they are out of your life all together? Do you loathe them so much that you can't stand looking at them anymore (even though deep down you really may miss them?) Whatever the case may be, it will likely take you a half hour or more to delete many of these photos, and that's a half hour of your life you'll never get back because you wasted it on Facebook de-tagging. Man, that sounds lame, doesn't it? And no offense, do you really think THAT many people are looking back at your old pictures? NO. They most certainly aren't. You're likely the only one who notices and cares.

If pictures happen to pop up on the sidebar of your homepage of you and your ex, then it may make sense to click in and delete, but to go out of your way to do so is just time-consuming, rather silly, and unnecessary.

If you feel you NEED to delete these photos to help you move on, by all means feel free, but don't go through all 987 photos tagged of you and delete every single one that includes you and your ex. At the end of the day, it's Facebook. Who cares! There are more things to worry about than these photos, I promise.

And finally, the biggest question – do I defriend him/her? And if so, when is the appropriate time to do so?

OK, let's break this down.

If you two ended amicably and there are no hard feelings, then there is no need to defriend. I will say, however, if down the road you happen to come across photos of your ex with the new flame and it gives you a weird feeling in the pit of your stomach, please defriend.

If you two ended horribly, screaming, yelling, and literally never wanting to see each other again – defriend away! If it was THAT bad of an ending, there is NO need to see what's going on in the other one's life EVER.

If you two ended on decent terms, but as the reality of the breakup sets in, it's harder for you to handle, then please defriend. Seeing their life on Facebook will only make it THAT much harder to really move on.

If you think you will see photos of your ex and a random cousin of the ex who you never happened to meet, and now you're making up stories in your head that it's a new significant other, and probably the one they are going to end up with, and now you're jealous, and thinking you may like them again, solely because now you "really" can't have them (and all along it was just a picture of him/her and their cousin at a family reunion), then DEFRIEND.

As well, if you find yourself looking at your ex's profile EVERY day taking note of their new "friends" and new wall posts, and literally having to force yourself to think that every girl/guy they are now friends with is some new hook up, or every wall post by someone new is someone flirting with them, DEFRIEND (and ease off, PLEASE.)

While likely all of this is false (and even if it is true, WHO CARES! YOU BROKE UP), you will be killing yourself over this.

So, at the end of the day, unless you really ended in such a great, cordial way (and how often does that REALLY happen), you should defriend.

Happy de-tagging!

What your Facebook profile picture is REALLY telling people

Now we are going to dig deep into the reasons behind why girls pick the pictures they do to represent them on the beloved

FACEBOOK (and what these pictures actually mean). It's not solely what meets the eye. I got some insights from a male friend, and I will warn you that this post is slightly harsh, but I never told you I was going to go easy on you. Take it away…

Ladies, your Facebook profile picture is EVERYTHING. Yes, guys are that superficial. Guys look to see if the girl is hot and if not, NEXT! If they like what they see, they will try and stalk your other profile pictures and regular ones, too.

The next option is to add you as a friend and hope you accept, so the guys can see more of your "portfolio."

Now for some tips regarding your profile pictures:

- **Posing Pictures:** These include the "side angle" picture (AKA, the "good side" picture), the "hand on hip," which could feature you alone or with your BFFs, all of which may be utilizing the "suck in trick." Guys know about these common tricks to hide your full package. If you are hiding something, they will realize it. Lastly, they think you look stupid doing these awkward poses.

- **Partying Pictures:** These include pictures with a bottle of champagne, vodka or Patron being poured in your mouth; holding Magnum Rose' bottles with sparklers; "The Rage Face"; you and your BFFs standing on some guy's table at a club surrounded by other guys and bottles. These give off the exact impression that you think it does: you are a party girl who is extremely vain and superficial and probably not worth pursuing. You will get some credit, though, that you are probably fun when you are drunk.

- **Revealing/Short/Tight Dress Pictures:** An "RST Dress" picture is great to look at it as long as you look good in it. Though showing some cleavage is definitely a good idea, showing your whole boob gives the impression that you are probably slutty. These dresses make the need for you to use one of the tricks mentioned above appear that much more obvious. An "RST Dress" also gives off the impression that the dress probably will not take a long time to take off (dual meaning here, ladies.)

- **Fancy Dress Pictures:** Elegant and nice to look at though unrealistic for your usual environment. Make sure you look good before going with this one. You will appear high maintenance, but guys will forgive that a bit if you look really good.

- **Bathing Suit Pictures:** Look your best. Pretend it's the Miss America Pageant. If you look good in the bathing suit, guys will not judge you, but don't think guys don't know about the "suck in," the "hand on hip" and the "arm raise" tricks. You should also be warned about more than one bathing suit picture in your profile roster giving the impression that though you care about your body, you are pretty vain and superficial and probably not worth pursuing. The bathing suit pictures are definitely hot and fine in albums, but no respectable guy would want to date a girl who is preoccupied in showing herself off to the world.

- **Modeling Pictures:** This is an interesting one. Were these modeling pictures professionally taken for a casting, or did you pay to have these taken for your imaginary modeling career? Guys ask themselves this question. If it's for the former and you look good, well done. If it's for the latter, though, that is extremely pathetic! In either case, make sure you look good in the picture and it is not too cheesy of a pose.

- **Black and White Pictures:** Sometimes this could be a nice picture, but it definitely looks like you are trying too hard. (See "Modeling Pictures" above.) Also, guys can't tell from this if you are tan or a pale ghost.

- **Winter Pictures:** Rarely will these be that good of a picture since winter outfits are not so flattering. Guys do love girls in boots though. You should definitely keep these for your albums provided you look good in them.

- **Pictures Wearing Sunglasses:** Make sure you look good because guys know about the "sunglasses trick," too, ladies. You are going to have to take your shades off at some point and show yourself. Nice eyes are an asset, so flaunt them if you have them.

- **Pictures Wearing Hats:** Not a good idea. What are you trying to cover up?

- **Baby Pictures:** Cute for a second, but guys want to know if you are hot! These pictures leave some mystery since they can't tell anything from them. If anything, it looks like a cop out or that you are hiding what you really look like now.

- **BFF Pictures:** These pictures are extremely confusing for guys. They can't tell who is who unless each person is tagged (rare) or you allow them to see other pictures of you. The last thing you want is to "bait and switch" a guy into mistaking you for your hotter BFF(s) and then be disappointed. If you are the more attractive of the girls—yes, they can tell—you definitely do not want to be mistaken for your less attractive BFFs.

- **Pictures with Guys:** AVOID, AVOID, AVOID! The boy looking at your picture thinks you are dating the guy in the picture, wanting to date him, have hooked up with him, want to hook up with him, or he's your brother or male cousin. Bottom line is it's too difficult to tell the guy's relationship to you and you will lose points. If you must have a profile picture with your brother or male cousin in it, tag him so they know you are still fair game!
- **Pictures with Pets:** Cute, but you should step it up a bit. Also, if a guy does not like your pet for whatever reason, NEXT! You should save that picture for a Mobile Upload.
- **Doppelgangers (picture of a celebrity that you "think" you look like):** Funny for a second, but should not be kept as your permanent profile picture. Make sure to pick an attractive celebrity if you post one of these. You should also be warned that the celebrity steals your thunder. They are the celebrity, so why publicly compete?
- **Company Logo or Event Flyer Pictures:** You have got to be kidding. These shameless plugs should be reserved for your status updates or Instagram profile pictures, ladies!
- **No Profile Picture (The Question Mark):** NEXT!!! Please don't waste guys' time.
- **The Perfect Picture:** Smile and look natural like you did not try too hard to fool whoever is looking

> at this picture. Guys know most of you girls have become Photoshop experts and self-tan yourself on the computers. That being said, looking fake is just, well, fake. Though guys are superficial, they do not want to pursue girls who are so obsessed with making themselves look good for other people. This shows you probably don't have much else to offer. They see through it. Be yourself and act natural for your picture. If you've got it, casually flaunt it. You've got nothing to worry about. A great guy will find you.

SMILE FOR THE CAMERA, LADIES :-)'

Getting the digits…or not

One time I was at a charity event with friends. It was a very good time. Drinks were flowing, a fun crowd was present – all in all it was a great night.

I'm ordering my next drink at the bar and a guy comes up to me. We start talking; he's somewhat interesting, good looking, and seemingly witty. I may have been three glasses of wine deep at this point, but I enjoyed the conversation.

After a little while, I go and meet back up with my friends and we're about to leave. As I'm saying goodbye to (insert name here) he asks to see my phone, goes to my Facebook application, finds him on Facebook, friends himself, and gives me my phone back.

Huh?

I didn't really know what to say so I looked at him a bit strangely, told him it was nice to meet him, and walked away.

The next day I receive a notification that (insert name here) has confirmed my friend request.

Interesting? I don't even know who this person is.

OH! RIGHT. Of course. How could I forget. It was the guy I met last night who friended himself from my phone.

Hmmmm.

I kid you not – this guy never asked for my number, but he continued to send me messages via Facebook almost daily asking for plans, to take me out, to meet up, or just to see how my day was.

I actually thought it was quite humorous.

Maybe I'm just an old fashioned type of girl, but if you're asking someone on a date, at least pick up the phone to ask them. (Maybe you can even get by with a text message!)

And what about GCHAT...oh you can't forget GCHAT.....

Being able to instantly speak to someone over the Internet or via a message over the phone is a great modern day invention. It really is. Fascinating, really. It can also be detrimental to relationships. Sometimes I truly wish snail mail was the only form of communication, as it was back in the day. It would make things way easier, less room for interpretation, and just so much more romantic.

Gchat – the foundation of a relationship these days (or the root of all evil)?

Coffee in hand (decaf for me – regular makes me jittery), computer on, signed into gchat, and ready to start the work day.

When I was working and living in NYC years back, gchat was pretty much the only form of communication during work hours, and understandably so – you can easily minimize the screen when your boss walks in. It's easy and can be distracting in a good or bad way, and it's way less time consuming than pulling out your phone to send a text. All that being said, it has also become the way relationships start, end, and everything in between.

Boys – no offense, but stop being so lazy! While it's a no brainer for you to gchat a girl when you're bored at work, and it's simple for you to gchat a girl for her plans, it can also be taking the easy way out. Chatty, fun banter back and forth is fine, perfect, harmless, but please pick up the phone at some point if you want to actually ask this girl out! Not to say you can never ask her out via gchat, but picking up a phone would be nice! I know it's 2015, but trust me, girls like a phone call.

The other problem is when you're in an argument, it may be "easier" to talk on gchat. It's "easier" to "end things" on gchat. It's "easier" to have serious conversations on gchat. I repeat – YOU ARE TAKING THE EASY WAY OUT. Grow some balls, please, and confront the situation in person or on the phone. Gchat is a cop out!

And ladies – don't get so "heady" when he doesn't message you RIGHT when he signs on, or if he doesn't say, "Bye," when he signs off, or if he's "short" during the work day. Let me lay this out for you plain and simple…boys aren't programmed like girls are. They could care less if we don't say, "Bye," or if we don't say, "HI," or if we don't message them on gchat. BIG DEAL. It's gchat! I know you've been there – you've liked a boy, been talking to him on gchat daily, and all of a sudden he's MIA. *What the hell – we have been talking all day every day for a week and now he just stops responding? What did I do? I thought we had good conversations. I don't understand.*

EASE, woman. It's called work (you know – the thing that takes place Monday-Friday.) There are a million and one reasons why he may not be messaging you this week, but was messaging you last week. RELAX.

This brings me to my next point: GCHAT ETIQUETTE – the dos and don'ts of that lovely (yet deadly) form of communication.

Girls:

- It's fine to initiate a conversation with a boy via gchat, but if he doesn't respond right away, please don't continue to message him five times in a row.

- If the conversation is flowing and then all of a sudden he stops responding…first, don't freak, PLEASE! Do not think up some "funny" comment to say (which probably isn't even that funny) to try to get him talking again.
- Do not, and I repeat, do not bring up serious topics on gchat.
- Do not allude to a serious conversation (especially not the "Define the Relationship" talk) on gchat.
- Don't say anything you don't want him forwarding onto his friends…on the off chance he does send it along, you'll be forever embarrassed (or just click "off the record" – fun trick my friend taught me way back while gushing over her new love interest.)
- Don't take anything too seriously – this is gchat, after all.

Boys:

- Don't ask a girl out for the first time via gchat. (Give her a phone call at least this one time, please.).
- Do not fight over gchat.
- Do not end things over gchat. If you're going to end things and break this girl's heart, have the decency to do it in person.
- If you're in a bad mood, busy, and/or don't want to talk, just don't respond to her for that period of time. (Or say, "Can't talk right now, sorry.") Don't be "mean and cold."

So, for all of you – gchat is fantastic (not sure what I would have done without it when I had a 9-5 desk job), but if used in the wrong fashion—i.e., picking a fight, bringing up serious topics—it can be a major problem.

Moral of the story – keep the gchat conversations light, fun, easy, flirty, sexy…and you'll most certainly be good to go.

And PLEASE, for all our sakes, refrain from using every emoticon option they have circa AOL 3.0.

Pour Her a Glass and Take Away Her Phone

I know you'll all be able to relate to this one.

DRUNK SEXTING.

Now, drinking makes people uninhibited. We all know that. And many times drinking leads to texts that you may end up regretting you sent the next morning.

I'm 100% guilty of this lovely past time. Pour me a couple glasses of wine and I used to say anything in a text. It really was NOT a good thing. Luckily, being more mature and wise these days, I don't fall into this guilty pleasure anymore.

One time, my friend decided to have a birthday party on a Wednesday. (Who does that?!) Apparently we forgot it wasn't Friday and boy, was work not fun that next day. That's neither here nor there, BUT the texting was just flowing. This guy I had recently met started texting me and in my less than sober stupor, I was just going to town. LUCKILY, I didn't say anything TOO awful (err – ok maybe a few things I wish I hadn't said), but looking back at those messages the next morning was definitely not enjoyable. I cringed a bit. (Don't worry. The boy took it like a champ. Sort of.)

My friends have all been guilty of this. Really. Almost all of them. So many weekends we would be out and one or all of them would say, "I know I'm going to regret this in the morning, but it's fine. I'm drinking." Apparently everything is fine when you drink. Who knew?!

Then the next morning I'd be on gchat and my friends would

say, "I just looked over my texts and (insert name here) legit thinks I'm crazy. Why do I do that?!" So we would have this banter back and forth about drunk texting boys. It's honestly a pattern. I used to have this conversation SO many times with SO many of my friends!

What I personally used to like to do, when I remembered, was to delete all my messages that took place between the hours of 10pm and 2am while out. That way, the next morning you wouldn't have to be reminded of silly things you may or may not have said to the boy you may currently be swooning.

I advise you to do the same.

You could also just leave your phone at home, but who really does that? My friend has joked about leaving her phone at home some nights, but then how do you ring a ding ding your boy late at night for a little bang buddy action. So, of course, she never leaves it at home.

You could also just have the willpower to NOT text when you're drunk. It took me a while to get to that place. Oh yes, it did.

The drunk text is an inevitable part of people's nights. Sometimes it works in your favor. (*Yay, he's coming over tonight! He likes me!* Note to girl: he's coming over for sexy time only when he's coming over at 2am.) And many times it doesn't work in your favor and you wake up with a plate of regret for breakfast. Oops!

Chapter 3

HOOKING UP LEADS TO SEX

It's so interesting – the term "hooking up" has not been around for as long as most of you may think. Our parents' generation doesn't even fully understand what this means. Some of them actually think it literally means to hook up – as in hook up an electronic device. Others think it means to hook up as in meet up with friends. Oh, if they only knew it meant rounding the bases!!!

Contrary to popular belief, girls use guys, too

So, boys, you think you're the only ones who can pull the "This girl has a hot, banging body, definitely don't want to date her, but I absolutely want to sleep with her." NO. You're all wrong. Girls have needs, as well. There are times girls like to have "no strings attached" fun! I promise.

Prime example: one weekend back in NYC I was out with my girls. One girl happened to bump into a guy she hadn't seen in about six months. They were attracted to each other six months ago, he took her on a date, but it fizzled. Why? Don't know. Don't care.

They were having a great time together on this particular Friday night, and while she knew (and told me): "I'm not feeling this, but he's so hot. I typically don't do this, but I think I'm going to use him. It's been so long. I've been in a drought." YOU GO GIRL. I was so proud of her! This was most certainly out of her comfort zone.

One thing leads to another, and here we were at brunch Saturday after Mr. No Strings Attached left her apartment and did the walk of shame (err – the stride of pride) from the ever-so-lovely Murray Hill. Now, THIS was good brunch talk if you ask me.

Saturday night comes around. We're out – drinking, dancing, at a birthday party of a friend of a camp friend. (What's new, right?) We're having a great time and my dear "innocent" friend goes, "Should I hook up with him again? I'm really not into him, I don't want to date him, but I do want to hook up with him. And I figure it's good experience – that way, when I find someone I really like, I'll be golden." I mean if she needs to rationalize it to go through with it – fine by me! So, she texted him, he slept over again, and there you have it.

Sunday Funday comes around and here we are – recapping our nights. My friend's boy proceeded to text and say he wants to take her out this week. HELL NO. She will continue to dodge this question until he gets the point. She doesn't like him. She JUST likes to play with him.

And the tables have turned, boys…oh yes they have.

When to have sex is always an interesting question in any situation. This next section needs no introduction beyond that.

To have sex or not to have sex…that is the question…

If you're a guy, we know you've been through this dilemma. And you probably know this dilemma all too well. You've taken a girl out on a few dates, had a few sleepovers, and hooked up a few times. All is going well. *When is it too soon to attempt to have sex with her? Am I going to look like an ass if I try too soon?*

Is she going to make me wait for months? If she is, I'm pulling the plug. I don't want to be a dick but I have needs, and how do I even know if I really like her or if I want this to progress without having sex?

If you're a girl, we know you've been through a similar dilemma, as well. You've gone on a date or two with a guy you think you may really like. You've hooked up, you're attracted to him, he is treating you well, and you are quite happy with the situation. *I really want to have sex with him, but I don't want him to think I'm easy. On the other hand, I don't want him to think I'm prude. If I want a relationship with him, I probably should wait a while, but then what if he ends it because I'm taking it too slow?*

Have no fear, dear readers, have no fear. Your questions are being answered right NOW.

Let's break this down.

Guys – if you really like this girl and by really like, we mean you could potentially see yourself dating her and really being with her, then don't attempt sex right away. If there is a chance you do really like her, you should be taking her on dates, making an effort, and initiating conversations (not just at 2am on a Friday.) If all of that is happening, wait until the 4th sleepover—and the sleepovers shouldn't start until at least the 3rd date—to try. When you do try, don't be forceful. (No means no.) If she resists, then do not try again that night (or the next morning, regardless of the "morning wood" taking place.) If she doesn't resist, then there you go! If she does resist, do not try the very next sleepover. Wait until two more sleepovers happen and then re-try (assuming you're still taking her on dates and are still into her.) Of course, if SHE hints to it, you're free to concur (and you should or there may be something wrong with you.)

Side note: If you do not like this girl and don't see anything happening with her, but do want to have sex with her, then feel free to try right away. She may or may not want to, but if you don't care what she thinks of you or what happens after that, hey, you could even try on the first date! Douchebag.

Girls – if you really like a guy who is taking you out on multiple dates and making an effort, playing the "prude" card will only get you so far. And it's just annoying. Totally understandable if you don't want to do it right away (as in the first couple dates), but if eight dates go by (and multiple weeks), what are you waiting for? Do you not like sex? OK, that's something we should talk about because that's a concern to me. Not saying you need to be a nymphomaniac, but sex is good and necessary. (It helps relieve stress and anxiety!) Are you waiting because you want it to be the right moment? All right, sweetheart, I will promise you there will be no candles lit and rose petals won't be on the bed. If the guy is smart, he'll play some solid tunes in the background. (Dave Matthews is always a good choice.) And that'll be it. There will be no perfect moment. So, stop overthinking it!

And to all of you – don't forget to use protection! No matter how drunk you are, please don't forget the condom. (You know it is right in your nightstand drawer.) None of us want any surprises nine months down the road.

It's 1:00pm on Sunday – why has she not left my apartment yet?!

Guys – how often do you meet a girl out at a bar, bring her home with you, hook up with her, fall asleep, and the next morning you wake up at 10:00, ready to say goodbye to this girl and enjoy your day watching baseball with beers and the boys, and she will not leave? Why does she feel the need to extend her welcome? All of a sudden, it's 1:00 – the Yankees are starting, and she is STILL in your bed. Mind you, she didn't wake you up with a job of any sort, so why the hell is she STILL here?

Ugh. Ugh. Ugh.

It's an interesting topic.

And I know it can happen the other way around, as well, so you're not getting off the hook completely, boys. I have most certainly had a boy in my bed at one point or another who has felt the need to cuddle more so than get his shit together and leave my apartment. *Uh hello – I have a day (and you weren't supposed to be part of it!)*

Girls – do not overstay your welcome. Do not assume he wants to cuddle, watch TV together, and hang out all morning. If he takes the lead in this regard, then feel free to go along with it, but if he does not – LEAVE. If he does not initiate anything the next morning, LEAVE. Do not make a fool out of yourself. It's one thing if you've hooked up multiple times and you know the morning after routine with this guy, but if you just met him last night, it's a different story.

And to quote a male friend of mine directly: "Ladies, sticking around for a while is not a good idea. Guys do not like it. We are sitting there praying for you to leave. It does not mean that we do not like you, that we did not enjoy the sex, that we are not going to call you to hang out again. We just need the space. We want to call our guy friends and brag (usually) about the sex we just had with you. We want you to not sit there in our bed forcing yourself to wait until the time you made up in your mind that it is acceptable to leave. Most importantly, we want to have sex with you again (usually) and we do not want more of a window to screw it up while we are both sitting there sober feeling awkward!"

Boys – don't make the girl think you want her to stay if you really don't. Don't just be nice because you feel bad. Honesty is the best policy. You can simply say that you'd love to continue hanging out, but you have so much to do and you need to get going. She'll get the hint.

The next time you meet someone out at night and he or she sleeps over; be mindful of the morning after. Yes, it has the potential of being very awkward anyway considering you made the decision to go home together once you were extremely inebriated, but try to make it as pain-free as possible.

And if this was truly a one-night stand on both accounts, skedaddle before the other person even wakes up! It can be mean, but why lead someone on if you truly have no intention of seeing him or her ever again?

Moral of the story: have every intention of leaving soon after you wake up the next morning, and if the other person wants to go to poundtown again, followed by a spoon session, then you're in luck! If not, get your booty up, dressed, and take that stride of pride home.

Nooners – friend or foe?

I didn't think this was such a common occurrence, but it seems it's happening more often than we think (at least back in my hay day!)

It's lunchtime and it's already been the day from hell. Your boss has yelled at you twice, you were put on two more projects on top of the two you're already working on, you're hung over, grumpy, and pretty much just hating life. So, you text your "bang buddy," meet at the apartment, have a quickie, get back to the office, and you feel GREAT.

NOW, it's time to start your day.

If you're the type that can make it happen quickly, with very little foreplay, nooners are the way to go!

Of course, it all depends on where you work in proximity to where your "bang buddy" works, in proximity to where you both live, and so forth.

If all these factors line up, more power to you!

No one at the office has to know what you're up to. You're taking a lunch. No big deal.

However, please just make sure you do not look disheveled

upon your return back to the office! Make sure your pants are buttoned and zipped up, your shirt is tucked in, your tie is on properly, and your hair doesn't look like you just woke up. And for you, girls, make sure your stockings have no holes in them (not sure how crazy your nooner got), your skirt isn't riding up, your blouse is buttoned, and you look as you did when you showed up to the office four hours ago.

The Starland Vocal Band said it best. And who said the 70s were never going to make a comeback?

Sky rockets in flight, afternoon delight...

Ladies first, PLEASE.

I'm trying to think about the most PC way to say what I'm about to say, but I'm not sure that's really possible. So, I'm just going to be blunt: BOYS, UNLESS IT'S ABSOLUTELY PHYSICALLY NOT POSSIBLE, YOU NEED TO LET YOUR LADY FINISH FIRST.

Now that we got that out of the way, let's discuss.

Being a girl, I can tell you it's really unfair and kind of selfish if the guy finishes first and just leaves you hanging. *Hi! I have needs, too!* I understand if it's just physically impossible for you to wait any longer, but you really should do anything in your power to do so if you can. Stop thinking about what's about to happen, change your thought process for not even two seconds; just let her catch up!

I have to say there were times I've just felt bad so I tell the guy to go ahead, but then you better be ready to satisfy your girl's needs soon after you finish! I know it may be hard to believe girls are as DTF as guys, but sometimes they are even more so. They want to get to the finish line, as well.

From a guy's point of view – "All guys just want to get off. That does not mean we do not want the girl to get off as well. Obviously we want to get the girl off; it's just that girls usually take much longer to finish than guys. We actually take pride in getting girls off and then bragging to our friends about how good we were in bed. After all, good street cred is very important. You should try to make a conscious effort during sex to be less selfish and stick it out (literally) a little bit longer so as to try and get the girl off. If you finish first during round one, go for a redo 20 minutes later and get her off right making up for the first round. Other alternatives if you finish first are to get her off other ways. Either way, make sure to get the girl off."

All right, ladies and gentlemen, I guess that whole PC thing really went out the window now!

In summary, just like you would hold the door for your lady, you let her finish first.

Manners 101.

As we all know, chivalry isn't dead – it is most certainly very much alive, even in between the sheets.

No excuses, play like a champion

SEX is an extremely vital activity to one's life. Not only for the pure enjoyment and feeling you get during it, but it relieves stress and anxiety. If you're not having sex these days, please, ladies, buy a vibrator, and men, there should really be no excuse. Sex is crucial for your health!!

OK, what I'm trying to get at is for those of you in relationships of any sort, there really should be NO reason why, in your 20s (or ever), your sex life with your significant other is not exciting. I understand – we all work or are in school – we are all exhausted at the end of the day, but please, please, please don't let your sex life suffer! Not only will you be losing out (mentally and physically), but your relationship could ALSO suffer.

If you're just not feeling as excited to be having sexy time with your boyfriend or girlfriend these days, there are ways to fix this.

You need to spice things up!

For starters, try new positions. Don't be shy! Sexual positions don't only consist of missionary and girl on top. How about doggy style, reverse cowgirl, kneeling, standing, the piledriver, the seventh posture, the rusty bike pump. (Yes, that's a real position.)

Yep, this list could go on for pages. Try these things! If you don't know what they are or how they work, research!

OR buy the handy dandy book, Position of the Day, (but do not leave it on your coffee table when your parents come over – I once had that unfortunate incident happen to me, and it was less than fun explaining why I was the co-owner of this very book, which, by the way, was a gift from a friend, promise!)

What about new places? You realize you don't have to just have sex on your bed or on your couch, right? How about the shower, on the washing machine, the kitchen table, on the beach, outside on your roof, on a pool table, somewhere (anywhere) other than your bed. Not sure if you're a fan of doing it in a public place, BUT hey, if you are down to go at it in a bathroom at a bar – more power to ya!

Roleplay! One of my friends and her boyfriend LOVE doing this. I have to be honest – I've never done the whole "I'm robbing your house and you're the cop about to arrest me" thing, but apparently it's a good time. There are plenty: teacher/student, boss/employee, doctor/patient, flight attendant/passenger, and so on and so forth.

Sex toys! Enough said.

And girls, buy some new lingerie. Of course, your boyfriend likely loves to see you in any thong and bra, but buy something even sexier. Surprise him. Pick him up from the airport (or just answer your door) in nothing but a trench coat and heels.

There are ways to enhance your sex life so you're always enthused when you're about to have sex with your significant other.

You're not 65 years old, and even when you get to be that age, there is still no excuse.

Going home together on the first night – smart decision?

This is something that has been debated between my guy friends and my girl friends on multiple occasions. Let me set the stage for you.

It's 10pm, you're at your friend's pre-game. You, as the guy, meet a hot, fun girl. You, as the girl, are seemingly attracted to this guy you just met. Everyone goes to the bar to continue the night. The two of you continue to hit it off and hang out almost the entire evening. Good work, kids!

Now, it's around 2:30am, and people are starting to disperse. The boyfriends and girlfriends are pairing off, the bang buddies are finding each other, and then of course, those going home solo are, well, going home solo.

You, as the guy, are obviously going to attempt to bring this girl home with you. You, as the girl, will toy with the idea in your mind for a few minutes (even though you're dying to go home with him). *I don't want to appear easy. I really want to play hard to get, because this guy seems like a good one. Has ALL the right parts. If I go home with him tonight, though, he'll probably never call me again and it'll be over. But I really want to go home with him.*

Ultimately, you decide to go with him.

And then what?

The questions on deck are as follows: when a girl goes home with a guy the very first night they meet each other (and likely have sex), does it ruin all chances there were for this to ever turn into something more? Does her lack of playing hard to get screw her over?

Here it is.

Girls definitely lose some points going home/having sex with a guy on the first night. This does not mean he will not like you anymore, but a guy's opinion of you will change slightly. Now we are not saying: do not sleep with him for weeks either. Guys like a challenge (to an extent), but do not want to sit around and wait forever (countless dates) to close the deal. Unless the guy really really really likes a girl, they will lose patience after a few dates and their eyes will start wandering again.

There is another case which frequently happens in NYC, however. Guys will want to sleep with a girl continuously without wanting to exclusively date her (the "booty call"). The sex is good and the guy likes hanging out with the girl, but she does not possess enough qualities from his "checklist" to move to the next level. (Girls do the same in reverse, too). It is almost impossible to elevate yourself from the booty call label once you're already there. Don't kid yourself, girls; the only way you will change this is if you guilt the guy enough and he ultimately settles. This will be short lived, however. Just the nature of the game!

If you just want to hook up with a guy and do not care what he thinks about you tomorrow; then, you should have fun and totally sleep with him the first night, if you want, without concern.

Be careful about the following though, girls: if a guy is thinking that you could potentially be somebody worth dating, sleeping with him on the first night will hurt your chances. He will most likely think you are extremely casual about sex and probably doing the same with other guys you go out with. Some guys will not care and just be happy you slept with them and immediately try and wife you up. The majority, though, will see this as a flaw and begin to doubt whether pursuing you is worth it.

In the end, if a guy really likes you, he will want to sleep with you soon after meeting you for the first time, but do yourself the favor and do not give in night #1 (but not night #8 either). See earlier story for more details on this, ladies and gents.

A "bang buddy" will always be just a "bang buddy"

It seems there is a little confusion. While boys tend to know that a "bang buddy" will always be just that—there are outliers, but we are talking about the majority here—girls seem to think that there is a slight chance of hope that one day it will turn into a relationship. (Again, there are outliers who don't believe this, but we are talking about the majority here).

I will admit – I have been guilty of said situation. There have been times I've slept with a guy consistently, all the while hoping it would turn into something more (even though I'd tell myself I'm fine with just having sex with this guy.) My male friends are the ones who had to knock sense into my head. "IT IS SEX AND JUST SEX. NOTHING MORE WILL EVER COME OF THIS. IF YOU ARE OK WITH IT, GREAT, AND IF NOT, BE DONE."

Words of wisdom from my male friend:

> Having a 'bang buddy' is truly an amazing thing. Having had several of them in the past, I can tell you it is a great feeling to go out drunk in NYC knowing that you are probably going to have sex no matter what that night."
>
> I would definitely be more confident when I would go out as a result, because I would not have to try as hard to find somebody to have sex with.
>
> Another benefit is that if I would go out and meet somebody else and hook up with them, I would not be cheating on anybody because I wasn't in a relationship.
>
> There are some drawbacks, however. Just as you are out searching for somebody else to hook up with at night, your "bang buddy" is probably doing the same. There are definitely times when the other person is nowhere to be found and they don't answer your late night text. Odds are they are banging somebody else that night and you are

not getting any (nature of "the game," kids.) Usually this just means you lost your "bang buddy" for the night, and you can pick up where you left off another night.

Something happens, though, after a while with having a "bang buddy." Somebody gets attached and grows feelings and wants a relationship. I have been in this situation EVERY SINGLE TIME. It is inevitable that sleeping with the same person over and over again will lead to feelings. Sorry, ladies, but you are usually the ones to crack first.

The problem here is that the concept of having a "bang buddy" means that you are basically using each other for sex without the label, rules, and respect of a relationship. Ever heard the saying, "Why buy the cow when you are getting the milk for free?" Girls are warned by their mothers to remember this line because once the guy gets you with no strings attached, chances are he will become spoiled by it and not want to invest in the next level. (I mean, why would he need to?)

It is near impossible to elevate yourself from being a "bang buddy" to a "girlfriend." It is true that guys are selfish and want to get consistent sex in their lives without the feelings; however, when a guy does finally get feelings for somebody, it will be for a girl he respects. No guy wants to date the girl who had no respect for herself and just slept with him whenever he drunk messaged her late at night; who he watched do the walk of shame countless times. (Guys do not want you to leave if they really like you.) Not a girl who he gloated and made fun of to his friends about; who he DID NOT RESPECT! Guys want to be proud of the girl they put themselves "in a relationship with" on Facebook. They wouldn't want to date somebody who they will always remember mistreating.

> If you have a "bang buddy," odds are the other person does not respect you in that way and probably will never date you. If you guilt them enough, maybe they'll give in for the short term, but they will still not respect you and probably move on sooner than later.

Moral of the story is to have lots of sex with your "bang buddy," but keep your feelings out of it! And if you can't have sex without feelings, then buy a vibrator. I really don't know what else to tell you.

So, there should really be no more questions at this point. A "bang buddy" is strictly for BANGING. Plain and simple. The chances it would ever elevate to a relationship are slim to none.

Get it? Got it? Good.

The dreadful morning after

Glass of wine half-full, empty condom wrapper, comforter on the floor – somebody (or should I say two people) had a lovely ending to their evening!

The sun starts peeking through the bedroom shades, your head starts pounding, and you look to your right and smirk because a cute boy (or girl) is sleeping next to you. You left the bar the night before with a hot specimen, they ended up in your bed, and it was a perfect ending to a fantastic evening. Good work!!

BUT now it's the morning. The truly dreadful morning after.

NOW WHAT?

Do we talk? Do we strike up a conversation about the weather? Do we go at it again? Do we cuddle? Do we make small talk about how fun the night before was? Do we pretend this didn't happen and quickly part ways? HELP! This is nothing short of very awkward.

How to handle the morning after is always a big old question mark. If it's someone you've never hooked up with before, it could seriously be the most painful 20 minutes EVER.

It's not like you know this person that well. Yes, they may have been in you five hours prior, but come on, let's be honest. This does not mean you KNOW each other. What on earth are you supposed to do?!

Yes, you may have had a lovely night with them – dancing, drinking, and flirting. But let me remind you – you were not sober while this was going on. You were on a high from life and from alcohol at that moment.

When day breaks, you're sober, likely hungover, and feeling very uncomfortable.

Some DOs and DONTs when dealing with the MORNING AFTER:

- DO pretend you're still half-sleeping when the other person wakes up, and just hope they quietly say goodbye and leave.
- DON'T cuddle…unless, ladies, the guy initiates it, but I still feel this is slightly weird since you barely know the person, and now you're sober.
- DO go at it again IF (and only IF) both parties seem interested in this morning activity – there's nothing more awkward than attempting to hook up again in the morning when the other person couldn't be further from interested.
- DON'T ask when you're seeing him again. (Ladies, let the guy initiate this.)
- DO take off the guy's clothes you borrowed from the night before if you slept in any, and change back into your evening prior attire.
- DON'T walk out in the guy's clothing. This is so annoying for them! Yes, my favorite sleeping shirts happen to be the ones I happen to have from the past

men in my life, but this is NOT a good thing. Guys want their shit back!

- DO gather all your things as quickly as possible, say you have to get going, and LEAVE.
- DON'T kiss goodbye (unless, ladies, the guy initiates this) – you hooked up once!
- DO pat yourself on the back as you leave his bedroom and confidently walk that stride of pride home

The morning after doesn't have to be as horrible as it sounds.

OK, let's be honest; yes, it does.

However, there are ways to alleviate the discomfort as much as possible. Just don't think too much into anything, realize you had fun with a semi-new "friend"' and that's all there is to it. Nothing more. Nothing less. No need to hang around all morning and assume you're getting breakfast in bed (because you're not.) Don't be delusional. This was solely for sexy time. If you happen to see this person again, GOOD WORK, and if not – WHO CARES.

Congratulate yourself on a job well done. So proud.

Interim bang buddies – what a novel concept!

Sometimes you just need to get your fill for a short period of time. Whether the reason is that you're waiting for your "guaranteed situation" to move back to where you live, because you need a distraction to get you over your ex, or you just are in a drought and need a couple weeks of indulgent sexy time, it's the INTERIM BANG BUDDY.

Interim bang buddies are really a great idea when it comes down to it. It's just for a short period of time, you go into it knowing you are not going to get attached and you want nothing to come of it beyond the obvious (for x amount of weeks), and you're getting satisfied, as is the other person.

Now, be cautious. While you say you're going into three weeks of awesomeness with no strings attached and strictly to fill a void in your life for x, y, or z reason, you need to make sure you aren't lying to yourself. The worst thing that could happen is you SAYING you just want sex with this person until the person you really want to be having sex with comes back into your life, BUT you actually are FEELING something more. This is not good. If there's a chance you could fall into this category, you cannot handle the interim bang buddy (and that's just too bad.)

I was talking to my guy friend about it. He thinks it's a great idea and has done something similar in his past. He had a guaranteed summer "fling" a couple years back, and she was arriving home at the end of May, but HELLO, it was only April at the time – he wasn't going to wait around for said girl. He found an interim bang buddy! It solved all his problems and held him over until this lovely girl came back into his life.

This is not the same person as your regular bang buddy. We want to make sure you are clear. Your regular bang buddy is someone you continuously play with, all year round (never dating, of course). The interim bang buddy is STRICTLY for a short period of time. It could even be someone you've never hooked up with – just someone who you know would be good satisfying you, someone you could "use" without feeling guilty about it, and someone you'll be done with soon enough.

Please note: the person you choose as said interim bang buddy should know what you're looking for. You don't want them to get the wrong impression or start making assumptions on the situation.

I know this may be a foreign concept to some of you, but I'm telling you – it's a great idea! If you need a distraction for a short period of time for whatever the reason may be, THIS is the way to go.

Happy times!

The 5am boot

So, this is interesting.

Sunday morning way back when I'm doing a "night before recap" with my friend. Great night overall – lots of good stories, but there is one that stands out because it's just so peculiar to me.

My friend met a seemingly good guy at a bar (not going to mention the name of the bar, as I wouldn't want to blow anyone's cover here.) Of course, she was there because it was the birthday party of a friend of a friend of a friend. Nice guy, a bit older than her, in his early 30s and very good looking. Yay, friend! Good work!

One thing leads to another and he gets her number; they continue talking, it's around 3am, and they decide to go home together. She was well aware she was breaking the cardinal rule of NOT going home on the first night, but she also was in the mood for some action and was kind of looking for what we like to call an "interim bang buddy."

She goes to his apartment; they talk, drink a bit more and hook up. (No, she did not sleep with him.) All seemed grand! All of a sudden around 4:45 in the morning, as they are nearing the end of their hook up – he asks her to leave. Yes, I'm serious, dear readers. He actually said, "Ok, so you can go now?" No room for interpretation there, I guess. But WHAT?!

I was very confused by this, as was she, of course. It's not like she was planning on extending her stay, cuddling all night, and talking about how she wants two kids, a dog, and a house out East. I mean she literally was there for sexy time. He CLEARLY was not having it.

I just don't get it. I've had boys over who I didn't really want to stay the night, but I didn't kick them out…I mean if it was nearing the late morning and they were extending their welcome, I'd finally say something, but at 5am? RUDE. We tried to dig deep into this one, but we really didn't get it. AND the guy was in his 30s even.

Maybe she wasn't as good as he expected? Maybe he was having stomach issues? Maybe he actually had a girlfriend (or a wife) who was coming home soon? Or maybe he just was over it after a couple hours? WHO KNOWS.

Regardless, it happened.

However, as I thought about it more (and I told her this) – it's almost better this way. What's the point in staying the night if the guy really has NO interest in you? There isn't really a point. Wouldn't you rather be asleep in your own bed anyway? Wouldn't you rather skip the stride of pride the next morning? I mean it doesn't sound SO bad.

It's one thing if a guy you had been consistently hooking up with decided to ask you to leave one random night, but with a guy you just met that night, I honestly think this isn't such a bad deal. You might as well know up front this guy will likely never call you and you will likely never see him again. Better to know sooner than later.

So, ladies – don't be surprised if you go home with a guy and you get the boot around 5am. If you think you may really like him, DON'T go home with him right away to begin with. If you don't give a shit and you wanted to use him for sexy time anyway, then you really lucked out. (No awkward "morning after" for you!)

OK, you can go now.

2 girls + 1 social circle = bad idea

A (male) friend of mine once asked my opinion on hooking up with two different girls in the same social circle.

I immediately told him he was crazy, but he reassured me they were both just bang buddies to him (and they were aware of their status), so it shouldn't cause any problems. I warned him this WILL cause problems because one of these girls is going to fall for him and then realize her friend has also been banging him, they will get in a fight, and all hell will break loose.

So, I did what any girl would do. I took a poll amongst some other male friends of mine...

> I have successfully pulled off hooking up with two (or more) girls within the same social circle. There are definitely pros and cons to it, but mostly cons. It almost never ends well and you ruin friendships. It has become more and more common for girls to not care about hooking up with the same guy. The fact is that if a guy is a catch, the friends of the girl (referred to as girl #1) hooking up with him will probably be jealous.
>
> Now, if the guy has good guy friends for the other girls, then everybody wins. Usually this is not the case though and the guy ends up running the circle himself. Competition amongst girl friends plays into the guy's favor as well. Typically in a group of girls, there are different levels of friendship: BFFs, close friends, friends and my personal favorite, frenemies. The guy should be wise to assess the friendship level between girls as the last two levels are the easiest targets. Drama will happen no matter which other girl he hooks up with though.
>
> Before going for another girl in the circle, a guy needs to accept and be ok with inevitable drama. Playing dumb or saying you were drunk will not work. It is definitely better if you have not spoken to or hooked up with girl #1 in a while. That way at least girl #1 can't say that her "friend" stole you.
>
> Guys must also be prepared that they probably will not be able to hook up with the girl #1 ever again once they get

> with her friend. (Exceptions do occur). There will always be some form of tension or drama going forward once the deed is done. Odds of dating girl #2 (or #3) will be slim to none as none of the other friends will be highly supportive.
>
> Bottom line, unless you like dealing with constant drama, think extra hard before hooking up with an old (or current) hookup's friends.

Well, there you have it. I highly advise you to steer clear of this situation. Nothing good can come of it.

There are enough circles of girls out there – go find another! But this time – stick to one girl within the circle, please.

Big spoon, little spoon

The cuddle factor.

Sometimes I just don't get it.

Why do guys cuddle with girls when it's strictly a sexy time situation (i.e., just sex)? Isn't cuddling for those who are dating, or at the least, hooking up on a somewhat regular basis? Isn't it not for those who are just randomly sleeping together once? I mean cuddling is an intimate thing in my book, and as much as I do love it, I think it's just straight up awkward to be spooned all night by someone you just randomly hooked up with for the first time.

Am I wrong to feel this way?

I really am pro cuddling, I promise. If you like the person and you've been hooking up pretty consistently and on a somewhat regular basis, cuddle away! If it's a boyfriend, of course, cuddle time is vital. (Although, there are times you'd rather just sleep than have your right arm go numb due to the position you are cuddling in.) If it's some "random" guy you're hooking up with one random night – don't spoon because it just seems uncomfortable.

I understand when you're drunk it may be a different story, and cuddling seems fine and not awkward because, well, you're drunk. What happens when you wake up, though? You're not going to cuddle sober and in the daylight with this "random" person you just spent the night with. It just adds to the morning after awkwardness. (Refer to the previous story.)

Here's the thing. If you don't like the girl, and have no intention of calling her or taking her out on a date, why the hell are you wasting your energy cuddling and giving off the wrong impression?

On the flip side, if you know this girl (and didn't meet her for the first time the night you took her home) and you do really like her and want to really pursue her, then cuddling is fine. I'll allow it in this case (to a degree.)

It's just such a funny thing to me. I know people like being held and "spooned," but when you're having a random hook up, it just seems so odd to me to "hold" this "random" girl in your arms, acting as if you care about her.

Moral of the story: be cautious when you're cuddling. It can send mixed signals and can also just be perceived as weird (and totally unnecessary) depending on the situation. If it's a random "one night stand," please, no cuddling.

The transition

You've been in this situation. Don't even tell me you haven't.

You bring home a girl or you go home with one – whatever the case may be. You're on the couch making out and in such an awkward position to really hook up. How do you make the transition to the bed?

You don't want to just say, "Ok, let's go to the bed," and you also don't want to "force" it if she doesn't want to. But let's be honest, you are so DTF it's not even funny – what are you supposed to do?!

There are a few ways to handle (or not handle) said scenario.

You can pull the "my neck is hurting" card and tell her it would be more comfortable on the bed, but that's just a bad lie.

You can say in an ever so sexy tone, "How about we move this situation to the bed," but that's just cheesy.

You can tell her that her bed looks so comfortable and you'd love to test it out, but that's just bad, guys – please have more game than that.

You can ask her for a tour of the apartment, and as you get to the bed, you can throw her down and just go at it… winning!

You can say you have to go to the bathroom and when you come out, just go straight to the bed, and hope she follows. (They usually do.)

But you also don't really have to say much. A head nod tends to do the trick. Really, it does.

Sometimes you can get lucky and the girl will take the reins because, well, she has needs, too, as we've discussed.

If you don't have the balls to take the initiative on the transition, and she isn't budging, sorry dude – you're shit out of luck and you've just gotten yourself into an all-night game of tonsil hockey (on the couch.)

Shoot. Score. Win.

Safety first!

We know none of you listened in Sex Ed class in 8th grade. Consider this an abbreviated, modern-day version (and a bit racier.)

There seems to be confusion amongst some people out there (don't worry – I won't be naming names) regarding "etiquette" and condoms. Should you, as the guy, carry them in your wallet in the hopes you'll be getting lucky that evening? Should you, as the girl, stash them in your dresser drawer or always assume the guy should come (pun intended) prepared?

Girls should definitely keep condoms at their apartments. Times have changed. Yes, a guy may initially think the girl has a lot of sex if she has condoms at her place, but not as much as he would have years back. Having condoms is definitely better than not. The guy will just remember that you did not have condoms and sex did not happen. At least give yourself the chance to advance to the next level.

Guys will usually plan to bring the girl to his place (fully stocked with condoms), but circumstances arise where that does not happen. When a guy shows up to the girl's apartment, he is ready for action, but unless he goes out with condoms in his pocket (uncomfortable and sort of sleazy), nothing is happening unless a) the girl has condoms or b) he awkwardly runs to a nearby store to buy some (huge buzz kill.)

Sex does not usually happen right when you get to the apartment, so neither party wants to be in the situation where sex is about to happen and there are no condoms. That is the absolute worst scenario.

I'm all about safe sex so you party girls who are on the pill and do not care about using condoms, calm down. Guys get freaked out when a girl suggests not using one even though it obviously feels better. Girls should "woman" up and keep some condoms at their place to avoid the aforementioned situations. Both parties will be thankful in the end (assuming the sex was worth it!)

So, ladies, don't feel like a "slut" (for lack of a better word) for keeping condoms in your nightstand. It's just about being prepared and ready if the opportunity presents itself and you want to jump on it (again, pun intended.)

Just because Aunt Flow came to town doesn't mean you need to leave town

That time of the month is never fun – for the girl or even the guy who she has been hooking up with. We're not going to get into the details of why said time isn't fun, but we are going to give some words of wisdom as to how you should handle it with your "bang buddy" or the like.

Let's start with something simple: just because you, sweet girl, may not be able to partake in all the sexual activity you want to on this very evening doesn't mean your man should suffer.

In fact, on the contrary.

Take this as an opportunity to give your man exactly what he wants and needs. Make him do no work for once. Tell him to sit back, relax, and enjoy. What a concept!

I know you're probably reading this thinking we must be crazy. *Me? Do all the work? I'd rather just cuddle and wait a few days so we can both enjoy!*

NO.

Sometimes it's perfectly fine, but every now and then, stop being selfish and GIVE to him. Really! You can make it fun. It doesn't have to be WORK. Use this as a time for some experimentation!

Now, those of you out there who don't let Auntie Flow get in the way of your sexual encounters, well, the more power to you. We will say, however, both parties involved need to be consenting adults. You cannot just pretend you aren't in the middle of that time of month, all of a sudden you're going at it with your man, and oh, hello HORRID surprise. No no – NOT okay. You and your manfriend, bang buddy, whatever he is to you – needs to understand PRIOR to engaging in sexy time.

So, next time Aunt Flow pays you a visit, don't be boring, and give your man a selfless treat for once. He'll love it and thank you later (in more ways than one.)

The daytime booty call

Now, I'm a big proponent for Sunday Funday. All my friends know this about me. I LOVE Sunday Fundays – brunch (with many rounds of mimosas), shopping, drinks, playing outside, and more drinks. And if you're one who doesn't get off the couch on Sundays – well, get out and enjoy your Sunday (after your hangover subsides, for you party animals out there!!)

This brings me to the daytime booty call. Of course, there is a possibility it can happen during the work week. (See previous section on "nooners.") But…this typically happens on the weekend.

It's Sunday afternoon, and a spell of "horniness" has been cast upon you, and you sext your "bang buddy!" Now, I know it's daylight and maybe you're not as drunk as you would be on a Friday night. (Ok, maybe you are.) But…I'm all about the daytime fun factor.

Whoever said booty calls and hook ups were only meant for the nighttime? There's no rule for that one! And if there was – well, rules are meant to be broken, right?

Now, we will forewarn you – if it's someone you've never hooked up with before or someone you've hooked up with only once (while very inebriated), be cautious because if you're not drunk during the day, this can be slightly awkward. And who wants awkwardness to dampen their Sunday Funday?

Not me!

If it's someone you're comfortable sexting and telling to come over for some mid-day action, then good for you!

It also helps with the "morning after awkwardness" because there is no morning after awkwardness! There's no morning after if it's mid-day, guys.

Winning!

It's a bang and run! Or a bang, hang—only if both parties want to—and run. Either way, it sounds kind of exciting, doesn't it?

So, next time it's 3pm and you're in the mood for some fun: the daytime booty call may be the way to go.

Saying Goodbye

I'm done hooking up, she/he is putting clothes back on and making an exit. Do I kiss goodbye? Cheek? Lips? Do we make out? Do I just nod my head? Do I wave? Nothing at all?

Oh the dilemma!

Saying bye after a hookup/sex is always an interesting interaction. My personal opinion is to just go with the flow, and sometimes it's rather entertaining to see how the other person handles the "later that night" or "the morning after."

Some guys may be fine kissing on the lips after hooking up/sex, because let's face it, there was a lot more going on earlier aside from kissing. Simply kissing the other person on the lips when saying bye seems neutral. Whereas, making out to say bye may be a little extreme, if not trying to date. Kissing on the cheek is almost like "thanks for the hookup/sex, and see you around." Even if not intending to date the other person, or if there are no real feelings there, kissing on the cheek is not the nicest thing to do when saying bye after a hookup/sex.

However, if the other person turns a cheek to you when saying bye, just go with the flow. They are clearly not that into you.

Now, for those people who just leave without anything at all, that is just ODD. That person is clearly feeling awkward by what he or she just did (probably drank too much – lucky you!) and is thinking too much about it and showing it. Just let them leave and do not worry about it so much. If they want to leave it that way, you owe them nothing. No need to get upset by the lack of manners. If he or she wants another crack at it, the ball is in your court. If the daytime bang does it again the next time, clearly there is an issue and you probably should not be hanging out with that person. Once is excusable, but twice is just plain rude. Say thank you for the hookup/sex and find somebody new!

Next time you hookup/sleep with somebody, think about

how the other person feels after the way you say bye to them. The way you say bye via kiss (or don't) can have a huge impact on whether or not you will ever get to say bye again!

Oh, summer flings!

Summer camp, lemonade stands, running through sprinklers, Slip 'N Slide; summer when we were younger was such a fun carefree time. And guess what? Minus the 9-5 situation it's still such a fun, carefree time. And one of the most exciting parts of summer once you're a bit older (err – I guess some of you may have been on the wild side as a young'un, as well) is the infamous SUMMER FLING.

Sun, heat (normal heat, not 105 F degrees heat), a fabulous summer wardrobe, bbqs, the beach…oh, I get goose bumps thinking about how much I love the summer season! Summer puts everyone in a significantly better mood, and I don't know how it goes down in other cities out there, but in New York, everyone becomes significantly more attractive once the warmer months hit.

Where are these beautiful men hiding the other nine months of the year? I mean, really! People literally hibernate in this city when it's too cold out. (I was totally guilty of this!) But…once the second half of the year starts rolling around, oh boy!

And summer flings just add some delicious icing to the cake. As we all know, most of New York City heads east, come summer. Weekends are no longer spent at three birthday parties a night downtown; they are spent in the Hamptons or Fire Island or by the shore.

I actually think they should rename Fire Island to Sex Island. Honestly (and more to come on this soon!) Some of my best male friends used to go there every weekend and would literally meet a new group of girls EACH time. It's endless. Sunday night recaps have gone from, "Yeah, I met this cool girl, we made out at the bar, nothing major" to "Three nights, three different girls – I had to sexile (insert name here)." I mean I really think they put something in your drinks over on the Isle of Fire. A horny pill or something.

Summer flings are a great great great situation. It's one of the best times of the entire year, everyone is happier, work is lighter (in most fields), summer Fridays are prevalent, and having someone to play with throughout this glorious season is just fantastic. For some reason it just seems like it's easier, more casual, not so serious, which makes the whole situation with this new girl/guy THAT much more enjoyable.

Don't get me wrong, I know a fair amount of people who have met their current bf/gf over the summer, at a share house, and it may have started as a summer fling, but three years later they are still dating! So, summer flings DO have potential to turn into something more, but don't go into it thinking that way or you'll ruin the vibe.

Summer flings should be handled as such: a fling! It's fun, it's easy, it's less uptight.

Girls – I'd advise you to NOT get "heady" when summer flinging. I mean I'd advise that all the times, but especially not when dealing with a guy you just see on weekends at the beach. Don't overanalyze. Don't over think. Just have fun!!! Come fall, I'll allow you to take things a bit more seriously, but in this short season – live it up.

Boys – I'd advise you to be cautious when flinging with multiple girls. For example, telling all the girls you're "seeing" where you'll be one night isn't wise because then all will show up and you've just entered the Bermuda Triangle, and we know nothing good comes out of that.

Sandy and Danny had it right all along.

Oh summer lovin' had me a blast, summer lovin' happened so fast...

The best kind of BFF

You know the movie *Friends with Benefits*? I have to tell you I am TOTALLY down for this arrangement. Years back when I saw this movie, I kind of really wanted a friend with benefits who would turn into a lover. Not such a bad set up.

But really, that movie got me thinking. It's such a fantastic idea for oh so many reasons.

For starters, let's say you come out of a relationship (serious or not) and you're in no place to jump into another. You need some time for yourself, to figure things out, and take a "breather." It is the perfect time for a no strings attached situation (similar to the aforementioned bang buddy we have discussed many times.) You don't want anything emotional, you don't want anything complicated, you don't want any feelings – just some fun with someone you enjoy and are attracted to on some level.

Let's say you have some phobia of commitment for whatever the reason may be – again, this is the perfect situation for you. There's no real commitment whatsoever.

Let's say you're just, well, horny. Again, this would work wonders for you.

Let's say you haven't had much experience in between the sheets and you really want to step up your game before your next relationship – ding ding ding – another great reason the "friends with benefits'" situation would be great for you.

Now, of course, complications can arise if one of the people involved with said scenario starts to have feelings for the other person. This can cause a headache.

For both people involved, before entering into this "friends with benefits'" territory – you HAVE to make sure you know what you're getting yourself into.

While it can be a wonderful thing, it can also blow up and be disastrous if you don't tread carefully. If you are one who gets attached the moment a guy enters you, this is NOT for you. If you are one who has a hard time separating sex from feelings, this is NOT for you. If you have had a "crush" on this person in the past, this is NOT for you because more than likely those feelings will come back.

So, make sure you are both aware of what you're about to start doing, and the SECOND (I mean second – even millisecond) even the smallest of feelings start forming on one end, you need to STOP. Like STOP immediately.

If, for some reason, feelings form on both ends, well then more power to you, and good work!

In conclusion, I highly recommend *Friends with Benefits*, the movie, but also "friends with benefits," the reality.

Tiptoe Down the Hall I go

Remember college? When you'd live on the 7th floor and your bang buddy would live on the 4th floor? It's 3am, everyone is getting back to the dorm (or this was also quite prevalent in certain college's apartment complexes, as well) from the bars, you change into your ever-so-sexy lingerie (err – his frat shirt) and you go to poundtown. Then you either would go back to your dorm room (or apartment) that very night—what a commute!—or the next morning. Clean. Done. BAM.

Well, in the lovely city of Manhattan there are those buildings that tend to feel like dorms. Dorms on steroids! You know the ones I'm referring to (ehem, those in the 30s on the east side...)

Many times when you live in one of these buildings, you know many other people that also live in them. This can be fun. Great actually! Lazy Sundays...you SHOULD be Sunday Funday-ing, but I understand sometimes LAZY Sundays are necessary...are easy when you can meet your friend on the couch for movies and wine. Or random nights in or even "pre-games"...all made so easy when living in the same building as other people you know.

What can be somewhat of a tricky (or wonderful) situation is when you live in the same apartment building as your bang buddy. I know similar situations happened in college all the time, but things are DIFFERENT post-college. Everyone is fooling around in college. It's like part of the "what you must do in college" handbook. However, in your mid 20s it's different. Things can get quite awkward if you "shit where you eat." Excuse the gross phrase, but it was necessary.

So, how do you handle living in the same building as the guy or girl you're currently sleeping with or hooking up with or swooning over – WHATEVER? Well, I'll tell you what you shouldn't do; you shouldn't start staking out the lobby around 3am every Friday and Saturday night. Hello, crazy!!

What you MUST do is remain calm, cool, and collected. You, by no means, are allowed to get "heady" and start questioning things. You two are in the exact same situation as you were prior to living in each other's building. You are hooking up, you are sleeping together, you are going on dates, you are nothing – whatever the case may be.

You can't start messaging this person MORE because of them being in your building (Well, girls – you can't. Boys need to initiate or they'll just be annoyed, push you off, and then that'll be a fun awkward encounter when you both happen to be checking your mail at the same time.)

You can't "assume" you're going to hook up every single weekend night now that you're living under the same roof. There are times HE may come home with some girl or SHE may bring someone else home. If you witness this, do not freak out, and do not carry on drunk in the lobby; go to your apartment and vent to your friends. This is to be expected. It would have happened regardless of you living in the same building or not.

Ladies, I'd advise you to not start decking yourself out before running to CVS if you hadn't done so prior (but why you did so prior I'm not really sure.) Don't change anything now that he lives in your building. That's silly and he'll catch on to that!!

Gentlemen, if this is a girl you know who likes you and you don't feel the same about (well, you feel the same about certain things – ehem, but not in terms of moving to the next step), then tread carefully, PLEASE. If your plan is to bring a different girl home every weekend, don't continue messaging this one 24/7 to make her feel she's still the only one in your multi-girl rotation. Because she'll only continue to like you more and then one day see you in the elevator with some broad you met earlier that night and that won't be fun for her!

It's not all negative, though! Really, it's not. I just wanted to warn you. It can be REALLY fun and a REALLY great situation. If both people are on the same page—whatever page that may be—it's great. Lazy night, rainy Sunday, drunken Tuesday, horny moment – and she (or he) is right down the hall. How convenient!

If you have to be somewhere or have an hour in between meetings or plans, it can be quick, easy, and efficient – bingo! If you're just bored – ding ding ding! So, this can be a great thing – truly it can be!

I just warn you to be careful and cautious. There's a fine line you don't want to cross when residing at the same address as your bang buddy (or whatever they may be to you.)

In conclusion, for all of you boys and girls who currently are in this situation or are going to be soon with new leases starting, old leases ending, have fun with this! It'll bring back the days of living in the dorms, but this time no RAs.

North, south, east, west

I was out to dinner with a couple of my closest girl friends a while back and we got to talking about men (shocker) and what to do when they just don't KNOW what to do.

And, yes, right now we're talking about in between the sheets, if you were confused.

It is possible that not every man is a stallion in bed. I feel bad for those that aren't, BUT don't worry, boys can be easily trained in this department. They WANT to make you happy and they WANT you to get to the finish line, so they WANT to hear what works for you and what doesn't (and if it doesn't work – how to MAKE it work.)

Hypothetical scenario:

You and your man are hooking up. It starts off with a steamy session of tonsil hockey. It leads to both of you wearing fewer articles of clothing than when you began the steamy session. It then turns into a full-fledged hardcore hook up situation.

YES.

However, he's just not there yet. He does most things right, but he just isn't satisfying you to the utmost degree at this moment. And, girl, you are stressed, you had a long day, and you JUST want to get to the finish line!!! Calm down and direct him. You're allowed to do that. Don't be demanding or forceful but gently show him where might work better or how it might work better and subtly hint to that by way of gently moving his hands, for example. He'll get the picture!!! Really, he will.

I've never been with a guy who DOESN'T like being directed. Some girls tend to think it makes guys feel less "superior" when you "help" them out. This is not true. It's not like you're telling him he's a bad driver. You are just helping him with the inner workings of the female body! Not all girls are programmed the same. What worked on one girl may not work on another. You are allowed to direct.

What you should NOT do is be demanding and forceful in an unattractive way. That will just kill the mood altogether. You also should not grunt and say things such as "Ugh, honestly you have no idea what you're doing." That will not only kill the mood, but also piss the guy off. And when that happens – nobody is getting to the finish line.

In conclusion, you are allowed to help direct men in this regard in order to help further satisfy you! It won't only help you, but it'll make the whole hook up situation that much better.

You may not be able to give a man directions in a car, but this is a time when telling him to go South may be beneficial.

Ready, set, go.

The Isle of Fire is Sizzling at No Less Than 500 Degrees

WOW.

The couple weekends I spent at Fire Island many summers back was nothing short of insane. What I was part of and witnessed could take up multiple chapters. Some things are not appropriate to mention, but I'll give you a glimpse into what transpired over a 48 hour period of time on the sizzling hot Isle of Fire.

Now, if you've never been to FI, you better make your way there during the summer months. Prior to going I advise you to be well rested, ready to hurt your liver for a weekend, ready to dance like you've never danced before, ready to make one or more bad decisions while there, ready to sweat profusely between the hours of 11pm and 5am, and set no rules for yourself (because rules are not followed on this island… anything goes.)

If you go, you will likely encounter one or more of the following:

- If staying at one of the ever-so-classy hotels—I like to call them hostels—you will feel like you're on your Freshman Hall at college all over again.

- You will likely witness boys (and maybe girls) running half naked through the halls.
- Shower buddies (Why create communal showers if you're not going to conserve water and shower with someone?)
- If staying at a house, you will also feel like you're in college all over again at a 48 hour frat party.
- You will likely bump into someone you used to hook up with, someone you're currently hooking up with, or someone you used to date (and then you will proceed to rekindle that awesome love affair for a night.)
- You will recognize many people at every bar: there are only about six that people frequent.
- You will bump and grind with a plethora of men or women, and sweat profusely while doing so. (FI bars don't believe in A/C, but it's all part of the program.)
- You will sleep maybe three hours each night.
- You will feel like you're on Spring Break in college when on the beach.
- You will go to sleep at 5am Saturday morning to wake up a few hours later and do it all over again for another day and night.
- You will end up with about five stamps on your arm each night from the inevitable FI bar hopping excitement.
- Someone in your group may go missing for a night, but they will arrive alive and well (and having been successful) on the ferry back Sunday morning.

- You will drink too many drinks (Rocket Fuel being the important one) each day.
- You will likely make out with at least two or three people a night.
- The dance floor at the late night bars will resemble something similar to a sex festival.
- You will likely wake up in your hostel room with your roomie for the weekend in the next bed hooking up with a girl or guy.
- You will likely do the stride of pride back from a house to your hostel or vice versa, and you may bump into a deer on the way.
- You may slap the floor dancing multiple times.
- You will jump up and down non-stop at most of the bars.
- You may leave the bar to have sexy time with someone and come back to the bar later to find your shirt on backwards and inside out.
- You will have one of the best weekends you've had in a long time.

That was just a glimpse into what goes on at a place such as Fire Island, which many NYC 20 somethings know well. Girls, if you don't want to go because you don't think you can "rough it"...if the people I was with can do it, you can, too. It's all part of the deal and you won't regret going. It's not something you'll want to do every weekend (nor do I advise that), but it's something you must experience. Once you step off that ferry on Ocean Beach, take a deep breath of the FI air, and you will now enter a weekend of craziness.

Chapter 4

DATING

You're not yet in a relationship, but you're definitely seeing each other. Similar to that grey area I speak of, but you're seeing multiple people. You're dating. One of the most exciting things about living in any city really. Meeting someone new, getting dressed up for the date, being nervous, maybe a first kiss with this person, it can be so fun!! And don't forget the morning after discussion with the girlfriends over brunch and mimosas.

Doorman Dating

Forget online dating – THIS is a newer craze in the world of dating, and it doesn't only apply to the buildings in Murray Hill.

Doormen know EVERYTHING about the people who reside in their building. They know our every move, our every EVERYTHING. It's really crazy if you think about it. They know when you leave for work, when you come home from work, when you leave to go out at night, when you come home from your night out, and most importantly they know if you come home alone!

Can you imagine the fun they have talking about every night? *Wow, (insert name here) is really getting lucky these days. Two different girls this weekend. It's the most action he's gotten in months. Props to him.* I sometimes think doormen should write a book on what they see and hear. It would be a best seller!

Way back, my male friend was talking to his doorman and jokingly asked if he knew of any cute single girls in his building to set him up with, considering he sees every person that walks in and out of the building. His doorman surprisingly said, "Yes," because apparently some single girls had asked him the same exact thing – wondering if there were any cute single boys to set them up with. His doorman asked what type of girl he was looking for, and a couple days later my friend here had three dates lined up for the next couple weeks! WAY TO GO, DOORMAN!

If you think about it, it's not such a bad idea. Your doorman is a trustworthy person. You wouldn't be meeting this person drunk out at a bar. You don't have to go online to meet them. You really don't have to try too hard to meet someone this way. Your doorman gives you a few numbers, you make some calls, go out for a drink, and there you have it.

I will warn you; however, dating someone who lives in your building – not always the smartest move. (See earlier stories for more details.) It can be great, but it can also be quite messy. However, I do have a friend who was once hooking up with someone in her building and it was the best of both worlds. She would still meet guys out at night, enjoy her night with her friends, and when she would come home, she just walked down the hall in her PJs. Pretty easy if you ask me.

So, if you live in a doorman building, feel free to ask them about singles in the building. Apparently you won't be the only one doing it.

The BBD

I was out for drinks with my friend one night, and we were discussing dating and how it's tough to meet someone you really like in the city. While you may meet someone who is great for the night or great for a date or two, it's not so easy to find that "perfect" person to REALLY date.

He brought to my attention his coined phrase of the BBD, the "bigger better deal." What is this you may ask?

This may not apply to all of you out there, but I know it holds true for many people I come in contact with. You are all searching for the "checklist," for what you've scripted in your head as the right person for you, the ideal candidate for your next big "love." The problem, however, is that because you are so focused on what this person MUST have, you miss out on those that may not have every single thing you envision, yet they may be the perfect person for you. This applies to guys and girls.... so, guys, if you're thinking this is about to get all sappy, it's not, and don't stop reading yet.

I know many people who have a specific description in mind of the next person they plan on dating. For example (and purely just for example): they have to work in this field (Finance), they have to be from this area (Westchester), they have to have gone to this school (Penn), they have to live in this part of the city (Gramercy), their parents have to be this (Lawyer), and so on and so forth. Unfortunately, those that think this way are closing out fantastic people because they don't fit their "ideal criteria" exactly.

They are looking for the BBD.

I met a guy one time who was good looking, ambitious, sweet, fun, funny, and a good kisser (always a major plus – *I mean I can't tell you how many guys just haven't mastered the tonsil hockey situation.*) I was stupid enough to not give him too much of a chance because he didn't seem to be the type of guy I would typically go for and had dated in my past. I kept dodging plans, he finally got the hint, and it was done. I probably should have gone on at least one actual date. You should give those "outliers" a chance.

Ladies AND gentlemen – even if he or she doesn't fit your

exact criteria you've ingrained in your mind, I advise you to give it a shot. The worst that happens is you spend a couple hours getting drinks with someone, you realize it's going nowhere, and it's done. In the scheme of things, it's NOT such a big deal! Let's be honest – what were you actually planning on doing on that random Tuesday evening anyway (besides *Pretty Little Liars*, of course?)

The next time you meet an attractive person, someone you seemingly click with, and who you have a good time with, DO NOT write them off just because they don't fit your checklist. Just one date – I promise, it won't harm you in any way. Go on one date, get yourself an adult beverage to ease yourself, and if it ends up being THAT bad, I give you permission to search for the BBD that very next night. Really, I do!

OK fine, if it's really that bad, I also give you permission to call up your bang buddy that very same night.

First Date: Dinner or Drinks?

This used to be quite the predicament amongst my male friends. Should the first date be dinner or just drinks? They don't want to offend the girl by not taking them out to a meal, but they also don't know how they feel about the girl and if they'll want to sit for an entire meal with her.

What a debacle!

Here's the thing, gentlemen. If you think there is potential with said girl—and I mean potential more than just late night hooking up when you feel like it—take the lady out to dinner. Doesn't have to be a swanky five star ridiculously overpriced restaurant because, no, that won't impress her; that might disgust her. A fun (not too romantic) restaurant where you can have a conversation is the ideal scenario.

If you know for a fact that this girl is STRICTLY going to be for sexy time, by all means, just drinks are more than fine. Sorry, ladies. Not to be harsh, but boys, why spend all the money, and sit through a lengthy meal if you have no intention of doing so again or really no intention of doing anything with the girl beyond hook up?

The dates I used to go on were a mixture of dinner, drinks, and some that start as drinks and turn into dinner (that's if they are going well, of course.) I, personally, was never offended if my first date was just drinks. I sometimes preferred that (oops) if I didn't know how I felt about the guy or if I wasn't sure if there would be a spark. One of my best (second) dates was one where we went for drinks (so we both ate prior) but since the date was going so well, we ended up getting an app and a dessert. We weren't starved, but were hungry enough to eat during our multiple rounds of drinks. Winning!

The last thing you or I want is slow service at a restaurant, waiting, and sitting over dinner with a guy (or girl) who you have NOTHING to talk about with (or just no interest in talking to.) It can be painful having to do so when you REALLY have no desire. If it's a Monday night around 9pm and I am stuck on a long dinner date that I'm not enjoying – I'm sorry, but all I could think about is *get me home immediately so I can watch my fix of the* Bachelorette – *I need to make sure she keeps my favorite this week.* Check, please!

In the end – it is up to you, boys, and what you prefer (because let's be honest you're the one who will be doing the asking.) If a girl doesn't want to see you again because your first date was just drinks, she seems too high maintenance anyway and you should move onto the next. However, if you are asking a girl out for just drinks, don't make the plan for 7:30pm. That is prime time week day dinner hour and then she will just be confused. Poor girl! Make it clear.

Dinner, drinks, it's all the same – just make sure you don't go Dutch on the first date. Based on principle, I won't allow it.

Happy Dating!

Are group hangs the new one-on-one date?

Apparently it seems that some boys out there have forgotten what a one-on-one date is. Not saying ALL of you, but it seems some have lost their way.

My friend was telling me how she met this guy at a bar. He approached her, they started talking, he bought her a couple drinks…all pretty standard if you ask me.

He got her number, said he wanted to see her again, and wait for it, he actually followed up! Sounds like a keeper, right?

He proceeds to call (not just text, but CALL) her and they talk for a while and he finally asks to do something a few nights later. She happens to be free the night he asked for, they discuss where to meet, and she's getting excited. It sounds like a first date is on the horizon.

Not so fast.

He then says, *Great – so a couple of my boys are going to meet out, as well. We'll all meet there at 8:30. Does that work?*

HUH? Rewind.

She obviously wasn't going to say, "No," after talking this whole time and agreeing to see him in the first place, but she was so confused. This was not a date anymore – it was a group hang!

She didn't know if she should be insulted or what. She had never experienced something quite like this before.

Hmm.

"Screw it," she said to herself, and she decided to just go with it. Why not, right?!

Fast forward to the night of the "date" – and it was exactly as she imagined – her new man friend from the bar last week, and his friends. Yup. It was a group hang.

She, with her positive attitude—this girl legit could have fun in a cardboard box—decided to make the best of it, and she ended up having a great time! I mean, why not? She was with a few really fun guys, and the one she had set up this "date" with was actually really sweet, funny, and overall a great guy.

One may think that this guy was just not that into her given the fact that he didn't ask her on a proper date. Well, think again, my friends, because they then went on multiple dates, and he couldn't get enough of her.

Don't worry – in time she did ask how on earth he felt it was OK to take her on a "group hang" for their first date (just to understand the thought process behind this one.) Apparently it didn't faze him and apparently he knew what he was up to, because, well, it worked!

So, in conclusion, dear readers, there are no rules. There is nothing set in stone that first dates HAVE to be like this or guys HAVE to do exactly that or he HAS to approach me like this and follow through like that. In the end, it doesn't really matter.

This girl went on a "date" that she couldn't have thought less of, decided to go for it, had the best time, and now she was very much into this guy and he was crazy about her.

Now I bet you boys are all going to rethink the first date situation, huh?

No awkwardness since your "boys" are there as buffers, don't have to KNOW if you like the person prior, no pressure – just a good time with good company.

Don't get me wrong, I always used to love a great "traditional" first date, but maybe group hangs aren't so bad.

I'm not opposed.

The group hang: the wave of the future.

Bring me back...

Sometimes I honestly feel that in my past life I was living in the era of *The Notebook*. And I used to sometimes wish boys would bring back the old days in terms of dating. I truly believe that email, social media, gchat, texting—while I'm all their biggest fan—I really feel they are the roots of all evil at times, too.

What about the days when snail mail was prevalent? Don't you remember the days when you would anxiously run to your mailbox after school excited to see if you received a letter with your name on the envelope? Well, neither do I, but I'd love nothing more than to receive a hand written letter from an "admirer" as opposed to an email.

How about drive-ins? I would love nothing more than to be taken to a drive-in movie theater on a date (with a bottle of bubbly, of course.)

Or a nighttime carnival, or dancing…(the options are endless.)

Or how about when boys used to pick girls up for their dates? Now, it's like: "OK, meet you there at 8pm." I get it – the city is spread out, and if you live on the UES and your date lives in the West Village and you're meeting in Union Square – doesn't REALLY make sense for him to pick you up, BUT I still think it's a sweet gesture when it works out.

These days it's texting instead of picking up the phone, and even before that it's: "Let's friend each other on Facebook because that's really a great way to see what this person is all about." UGH.

I truly believe if it weren't for gchat conversations, text banter, Facebook wall postings, and email…there wouldn't be as many fights between guys and girls.

Girl: Who is (insert name here)? I don't get why she's outwardly flirting with you on your wall.

Boy: Ease – it's my best friend's sister and she was joking.

(Now, the girl feels dumb.)

Girl: Why are you being cold?

Boy: I'm not. I'm at work, where I'm supposed to be at 10am on a Tuesday. Sorry, I cannot get into this via gchat.

Girl: Whatever.

(Girl is driving boy mental, and now he goes on invisible.)

Girl: So, what are we doing tonight?

Boy: Don't know. Watching the game right now.

Girl: OK, so are we not seeing each other tonight? I thought we had plans.

Boy: We do, but I'm watching the game. I'll talk to you when it's over.

(Girl now complains to her girl friend because her guy is being "rude" via text, when really it's because he's watching an important baseball game and doesn't want to be distracted until it's over.)

These are just a few examples of what can transpire via these modes of communication. Girls and guys think it's much easier to say things in this form, as opposed to face to face. I, personally, feel if it weren't for emails, texts, and the like – things would be very different with an ex and me today. Damn it, modern day technology!

Anyway, my point is that you boys should really try to bring the good old days back in some form or another. Get creative on your dates! Treat the girl as Noah treated Allie in *The Notebook*. Go find the nearest drive-in movie. Go out of your way to pick up your girl for a date. Or how about the easiest? Pick up the phone and CALL her sometimes as opposed to just shooting her a text.

It never hurts to switch things up a bit. Your girl will be impressed, I promise.

Ch-ch-ch-changes…

(Think "David Bowie.")

And with a click of your mouse…

How lazy have we gotten, people? You honestly don't need to leave your apartment for days straight and not only can you have all your food and meals delivered, bottles of wine delivered, dry cleaning delivered, movies on demand, but you can also find yourself a date without leaving your couch.

Online dating has been THE thing for a while now. It's honestly like a bar in your apartment. Make yourself a cocktail or crack open a brew, sign into your online dating site (or app) of choice, play some great music, and hello Tuesday evening excitement!

I truly believe, soon enough, the majority of people out there will be meeting this way. Apparently, along with Tom Hanks and Meg Ryan (*You've Got Mail*), I was ahead of the times, as well. Not only did I meet someone who I got into a serious relationship with on one of the ever-so-lovely online dating sites, but my brother and uncle both met their wives that way, as well. And the list goes on…

Some of my friends are having a field day being on one of the sites. One of my friends honestly has one to two dates each week with guys she meets this way. She is having the BEST time (and always reports back some good stories.)

It's an interesting concept – you're forming a "relationship" over a website full of people looking for that next significant other (sometimes in the form of an "activity partner," sometimes in the form of an actual relationship.) At first it can be a very superficial experience. You message people (or respond to people's messages) solely based on their pictures, followed by what they have written in their profile to hopefully make them stand out amongst the rest.

The picture can be a problem, though. Back in the day when I was on a dating site, I would see pictures of some very good looking boys, agree to meet for a drink after talking for a bit, and they did not look a single thing like their online profile pictures. I'm sorry – I know it's not all about looks, but to not look a thing like you do in your picture – that's just a LIE! What? Do you think the girl isn't going to realize you don't resemble AT ALL that one good picture you took within the 26 years of your life because it just happened to be on your one good hair day at your aunt's wedding a couple years ago. I mean honestly – girls aren't that dumb!

So, one piece of advice if you're doing the online dating thing or plan on doing it – only post pictures that really look like YOU. I understand you want guys or girls to think you're so "HOT" and to want to message you right away, but it's a slight disappointment (and just rather annoying) to show up to the date and be totally thrown off.

Another piece of advice would be to not make your profile so "cheesy." I remember coming across (and my friends who are currently online dating have told me, as well) some extremely "cheesy" profiles. Look – it's great that you're a romantic and love walks on the beach, and are looking for your soul mate and everything in between, but save it for another day. I know I speak for others when I say, I would get slightly turned off (and nauseous) when reading such things. Don't get me wrong – I love a romantic guy as much as the next girl does, but no need to point this out via your online dating profile. Your profile should be witty and funny and enjoyable to read, and NOT too lengthy. Tell the world about a few of your interests, some likes/dislikes, and keep it light!

One more piece of advice for the guys out there doing the whole online thing – when you're talking to a girl, don't talk to her for 6 weeks and then ask her out. Not saying you need to ask her out the night you start talking to her, but after a few days or a week of emails back and forth, it's time to step up your game, get her number, ask her out.

I am certainly PRO online dating for others. It's something different, it can be fun, you can meet great people, and it's just another outlet to meet men and women. Why not?! I mean you can only meet so many people drunkenly out at bars.

Whether it's match.com, JDate, eHarmony, Coffee Meets Bagel, Tinder, perfectmatch.com, okcupid.com, harvestdating.com (really – this one does exist), millionairemate.com or any site in between – find the one that best suits you and rock it. Don't be ashamed you're doing the whole online dating thing! I mean, I'll admit, when I was dating a guy from the online world a while back, we definitely used the "we met through a mutual friend" card at the beginning, but in time we embraced it. So, you should, too!

Next time you're not in the mood to go out, pour yourself a cocktail, get comfy on your couch, and with a click of your mouse, you have officially brought the bar and the boys (or girls) to you.

The Overshare

Now, first dates can sometimes be (err – most of the times) nothing less than super awkward. Don't get me wrong – GREAT things can come from first dates, but this doesn't mean all first dates are something you write home about. Sometimes people just don't know when to shut the heck up.

I was on a girls' getaway weekend, and you can only imagine the conversations that took place during said weekend. Well, I'm sure you can imagine. Sex, boys, sex, boys, sex, jobs, boys, and sex. Or something like that.

One of my dearest friends was telling us about a recent first date she had. This was a set up through a coworker. Standard situation, right? He seemed like a nice, good looking guy, and their mutual friend only had good things to say about him. My friend figured, why not?!

Well, the date started – seemed like it was going fine. They were just getting drinks. Painless.

Until he did "THE OVERSHARE." Why, boys, why?! There are times you should just stop talking and listen or at least think about what you're about to say.

This boy did 3 BIG TIME "NO NOs."

For one, he brought up his ex-girlfriend not even half way through the date. You just can't do this. The EX files should not be opened until many dates in. There is no reason. If you're still hung up on your ex and heartbroken; maybe you shouldn't be dating yet to begin with. If you're totally over your ex but just feel it's a nice conversation to have out there, well you're wrong and you need to go see someone about that. DO NOT BRING UP THE EX.

My friend was so totally confused and didn't know how to respond. *Great, your ex sounds wonderful – let's all meet for brunch on Saturday.* Ok NO.

So, that was rule #1 he broke as part of the OVERSHARE.

He then proceeded to say the following: *I was looking at your Facebook page and noticed your friends with (insert name here) who is friends with (insert name here) who is my best friend's sister. That's so crazy! Such a small world.*

Ok, rewind, ignorant boy. You just blatantly told this girl you stalked her. No ifs, ands, or buts. You stalked her and you admitted it. Now, it's one thing to "cyber stalk" someone before or after a first date, but to admit that to them – WHEN IS THAT EVER OK?!!! Not on Planet Earth.

And finally, the poor boy did one of the ultimate NO NOs when on a first (or even second, third, fifth) date. He talked about their future! Yes, he talked about the future with my dear friend on their very first date.

He proceeded to tell her that if they make it to a three month anniversary, they definitely owe (insert name here) drinks (meaning the person who set them up). All right, if you want to have these crazy thoughts in your head after only one date, go right ahead (although, that's slightly nuts), but you cannot under ANY circumstance mention these thoughts to the person you're on the date with. They will think you've gone cuckoo. Of course, this boy was only trying to make a silly, lighthearted joke, but this was not the way to go about it.

Moral of the story: be careful when it comes to THE OVERSHARE. I get it, you like to talk, and that's great. It could lead to a great first date. Just don't talk about topics you shouldn't be talking about. You're smart – think before you speak. And if alcohol makes you word vomit a bit, then please keep it at a one to two drink maximum while on this date. You don't want to say or do something you may regret. If you're questioning even slightly whether bringing up a certain topic is OK, more times than not – it will NOT be ok. So, zip the lips and bring up something else.

If you continue taking this person out on dates and things progress, then one day down the road there will be a time and a place for these conversations, I promise. And in the meantime, as per usual, keep it LIGHT.

Undershare trumps overshare.

Oh, the good old days

One of my best friends and I used to always joke that we hit our prime in middle school. I guess I shouldn't be admitting to such a thing, but we really LOVED our middle school days. Looking back, it was such an easy time. No stress, no pressure, nothing to worry about except what shoes to wear with our 3 inches above the knee plaid skirts. (We had to wear uniforms.) Typically, I'd choose my black Rebels – if you ladies never went through a "rebels" phase, oh boy, did you miss out!

What was "stress" to us back then was if we were going to be able to sit next to our crush at the lunch table! *Ooooh (insert name here) is walking in – I hope he comes and sits by me. I want to share my Lunchables with him!*

And then, of course, you would then write all about it in your diary.

Our Friday nights consisted of going to someone's house and playing "Spin the Remote" and "Truth or Dare." Things certainly got scandalous when the remote landed on our crush and he/she had to HUG us or kiss us on the CHEEK. Wow!!!

What can be really fun and unexpected is when you reconnect with an ex or a crush from those lovely childhood days.

Granted, both people would have likely changed a great deal almost 15 years later, but there's something about a childhood girlfriend or boyfriend. The relationship is so silly and somewhat pointless back then. (I mean what does the relationship consist of besides passing notes to each other in class?) But it's still fun and can be just as exciting for the person as a relationship in the 20s.

Don't rule out those guys or girls you may have once "dated" or swooned over back in the 6th grade. You never know when they may pop back into your life! It's actually a great situation because, while on one level, you are getting to know each other all over again (which is very fun), it's relatively "old," as well. You already know each other's families. You already know the "nitty gritty" about each other, and it's more just catching up on the past ten years and learning new things about the person!

You have likely shared many memories with this person and still know many of the same people, but now you're 25, and it's a much bigger deal than the days of "7 Minutes in Heaven." Kissing your middle school boyfriend at 25 years old doesn't leave you with anything less than the same butterflies you felt back when you were 12. But now instead of passing notes, it's text messaging. Instead of "Spin the Remote," it's having adult beverages. Instead of kisses on the cheek it's, well, a lot more than 1st base.

I, personally, feel reconnecting with an ex from back in the day is a fabulous idea. While I'm not all for reconnecting with a recent ex, this is very different.

One thing that will never change 12 years later is the calling of your best childhood friend and talking all about your crush. It's like no time has passed at all! Except now it's more than *Oh my gosh – (insert name here) just signed onto AOL. What do I say to him?*

Now I'm in the mood to go listen to some Spice Girls and watch *Full House*. Who is with me?!

If ya wanna be my lover, you gotta get with my friends...

Chapter 5

RELATIONSHIPS

I have friends in very serious relationships – as in very serious on the verge of moving in together and then getting engaged. I have friends who are married and probably having kids soon. I have other friends in more casual relationships, and I have other friends who couldn't be more single. I see it all. I hear it all. Relationships can be incredible, wonderful, amazing things. They can also be stressful, especially when it may not be the right one, yet you don't want to see that. What about the beginning of the relationship? You know, the grey area – the undefined. It can be the most exciting time, but also the most innerving. This leads me to…

I'm just DTF, not in the mood to DTR

It's a random Tuesday night, you and your "grey area" are hanging out (after the girl of this "grey area" forced the boy of this "grey area" to watch *Pretty Little Liars*, and yes the boy did like it but won't admit it). You (as the girl) have a bit of an "attitude," and this "attitude" has been going on the entire evening. You (as the boy) notice it, but pray it's just because she had a bad day at work because you do not feel like dealing with it. She's being short and not smiling. UGH, HOW ANNOYING.

Finally, you cave in and ask her what's up. (Yes, she's been dying for you to ask this all night). Girl says, "Nothing." OBVIOUSLY IT'S NOT "NOTHING." How stupid! I mean, I have to admit; being the girl, I've said "nothing" when it's really a big something. Why do we do this, ladies? Why, oh why?! If something is wrong, either tell your guy what's up from the get-go, or as soon as he asks – at least honestly answer. Boys are not in the mood for this stupid back and forth – it's inefficient and dumb! There are times to "play dumb" because it's effective, THIS IS NOT ONE OF THEM.

Let me go back a minute. You've been "seeing" this girl for about six weeks. You likely haven't been hooking up with anyone else because you do really like her, but you aren't ready for a relationship, you don't want the title "boyfriend," you're happy how things are, no pressure – why fix it if it ain't broken, right?

You know she's being like this because she's starting to wonder WHAT YOU ARE. She hates the grey area. You love the grey area (at least for right now.)

So, she starts alluding to the DTR (define the relationship) talk. And now you really wish you hadn't asked her what's wrong. You're so annoyed. You'd rather be at work right now, studying Excel documents than dealing with the DTR talk. You have been dreading the DTR talk. Well, here it is – staring at you in the face. Can't escape now.

So, you do it. you give in and have this talk. You tell her you're not seeing anyone else, and 10 minutes later you are…wait for it…a BOYFRIEND. Your newly esteemed GIRLFRIEND is thrilled. Her mood drastically changes, and all is grand in her life. You are thinking "what the hell did I just get myself into?"

And so it goes.

Some advice:

Ladies, try to hold off on the DTR talk as long as you possibly can. When he's ready for that talk, it'll happen. I promise it will. The more you poke at it, and push it, the less likely he'll want to be with you in that way. It'll happen over time. Just be patient!! If you're not patient, the following will happen: you will force the talk, it'll take place, he'll agree, a week later he'll start acting weird, you'll get in a fight, and he'll explain he just isn't ready for a relationship. It doesn't mean he doesn't like you but he's just not ready for that step. He's feeling pressured for no reason now, so you will have to revert and go back to the "grey area" which makes you question everything, and so forth. What you don't understand, ladies, is that he may really like you and only want to be with you (and no one else), BUT just the word "relationship" or "boyfriend" scares him. Why? It's a guy thing, don't question it – it is what it is. At the end of the day, it's semantics. WHO CARES WHAT YOUR TITLE IS? If he likes you, and you like him, it's all that matters.

Gentlemen: you need to understand that while not all—yes, it's true I have friends who HATE the talk..hate, hate, hate it, I bet you want their numbers don't you? —but many girls like and need this talk at some point. It's unfortunate, but it's true. That being said, don't make the poor girl wait eight months for it. You'll drive her crazy. If you aren't going to ever want to have this talk because you don't like her THAT much, don't lead her on. Please don't do that! And if you do like her a lot, but still don't want the talk – that's fine, too. (Half the time, the talk ruins things anyway.) But…make sure she knows you like her. Actions speak louder – no need to tell her all the time, but just make sure she knows!

Piece of cake.

Your boyfriend's best (girl) friend: yes, it's possible they are JUST friends

This is a subject I know about all too well. So, ladies, if you happen to find yourself dating a guy who has a best friend who happens to be a girl, I advise you to listen to me. Yes, stop whatever else you're doing and listen up.

Even though in the ever so famous movie *When Harry Met Sally* the characters debate if men and women can be friends without sex getting in the way, and ultimately Harry and Sally end up together – this is not so often the case in real life. Really, it's not!

It is very possible for a girl and a guy to be friends, and strictly be JUST friends without sex getting in the way. They may have been friends since childhood, maybe they only met two years ago, but if your man chooses to be with you and date you, you need to trust that his female friend is JUST a friend.

While, yes, there are times that a guy has a best girl friend who he secretly wants to date (or have sex with), if he is dating you (or having sex with you) currently – he doesn't want to be with her!

So, if your current boyfriend has a female best friend, you need to play it cool. You need to trust him. You need to let them hang out without you. You need to not freak out the second she calls or texts him. You need to not be rude to her. You need to not pick fights with your boyfriend about this. I promise he will get annoyed and question why you can't just believe him that he and his best friend are JUST friends. Ultimately, you need to RELAX.

And here's why.

If your boyfriend wanted to be with this girl and she wanted to be with him, wouldn't they have been together already? And they haven't even attempted it (or maybe they have and realized it was a mistake, so that's out of the way) for whatever the reasons may be. They may love each other, but just as FRIENDS. They may care for each other a lot and would do anything for one another, but wouldn't you do the same for your best friend (whether it is a guy or girl?)

Yes, I understand it's hard to imagine that there is another female in your man's life, besides you, that he cares deeply for (of course, aside from his female family members), but you've got to just accept it. If you want to be with your boyfriend, you have to accept him for exactly who he is and what he's all about (and this may include a female best friend!) If you don't trust him, that's another story and you should probably figure out what the real problem is, and it's likely not the harmless best girl friend.

On the off chance your boyfriend is going to run off with his best friend and date her, then so be it. Let it happen. And if that is the case, it wasn't meant to work with you and you need to move on…and fast.

There is no point to stress over something that is out of your control, silly girls! If they are going to fall in love, then they are going to fall in love, and that would certainly happen regardless of your freaking out over the situation and, trust me, they likely aren't going to fall in love at this point.

I can guarantee if you make a big issue over the situation, it will end up in a fight, and maybe even a break up (depending on how nutty you get on the matter…yep, guilty!) If it's something that seriously bothers you and you can't keep it in, then calmly explain yourself to your boyfriend, let him explain his side, and move on from it!

I will say, however, if your boyfriend starts hiding things from you regarding his friend or lying about his plans with her, that's a whole different issue and you should probably address it. Likely, this isn't the case, and if it is, it's only because he feels he needs to "lie" to you because he knows you get "mad" when he hangs out with her.

Moral of THIS story: trust your boyfriend, do not think twice about his best girl friend, and learn to pick your battles (and this should NOT be one of them.)

I know Billy Crystal (Harry) and Meg Ryan (Sally) had a unique friendship/relationship, but I'm telling you – you likely won't see your boyfriend and his best (girl) friend singing "Surrey With the Fringe on Top" in Sharper Image any time soon.

3 Bs – Boys, Business Time, Bathroom

One of my friends had been dating her boyfriend for about a year, and this boyfriend is probably TOO comfortable when it comes to the bathroom. He goes with the door open, he tells her when he is about to go, he doesn't cover the smell, and so on and so forth.

My other friend said her boyfriend of a year and a half is pretty comfortable with the matter. He tells her when he is about to go, but he keeps the door shut, turns on the water to hide the sound, and hides the smell afterwards.

My other friend said her boyfriend of a few months is not super comfortable just yet. He doesn't hide it completely (he makes it clear when he has to go), but he's not THAT open about it yet either.

When are you, as the boy, allowed to cross this line? When are you allowed to do your business in your girl's bathroom?

This is NOT something you do within the first few dates or even the first month or so. You need to be 100% comfortable with your girlfriend first and in a great place with her. If there's even a question regarding how she feels about you (in the early stages), you doing your business in her bathroom isn't going to make her want to jump your bones. No offense.

However, once you are comfortable with her and you are on the road to "more serious," feel free to use her bathroom for said activity. She knows you have business to take care of. She knows you're human. She likely has a father, brother, male cousin, best friend, and she's not in the dark ages. She knows you aren't going to run downstairs to the nearest Starbucks EVERY time you sleep over. Let's be honest here.

Now, I will say, you MUST shut the door. Living in the city, the apartments are not massive, and many apartments have the bathroom in the bedroom or adjacent to it. We don't have much space to work with. SHUT THE DAMN DOOR. Thanks.

Next, please turn on the water. No one wants to hear you. Honestly. Not necessary. She knows you're going in there to do business; turning on the sink water will help her to not have to HEAR what she knows you're doing.

Finally, PLEASE cover the smell (or try to.) It's called matches. It's called air freshener. Something. Don't just leave the smell there for her to deal with when she goes and brushes her teeth five minutes later.

We're glad you're comfortable with us, we really are! You just need to be courteous when taking this next step.

The LDR - pro or against?

Most people I know have either been in a long distance relationship (LDR) or have attempted one. Sometimes it works just fine and other times it's pretty much nothing short of actual hell.

He's there, you're here or she's here and you're there – you want to make it work, but sometimes it's just not possible.

Certain people almost prefer LDRs because they are able to have their independent life more than half the time, and every month or so they get to see their significant other. They like not seeing their bf/gf so often because the times they do see each other are that much better and that much more exciting. They also may be so busy with work and life that it's just not the best time to have a bf/gf "in their face" at all times at the moment.

However, some people cannot make it work. Those girls or guys that are the needier types (or jealous, insecure types) have trouble with such a relationship. Seeing their significant other once a month or every six weeks is NOT enough. No amount of phone/Skype sex could ever make this work for them.

If you are needy, dependent, have a wandering eye, worry that your other half is always out cheating on you, and don't believe in any sort of phone/Skype/text sex (sext) situation, an LDR is likely not for you.

If you are independent, busy, loyal, trusting, and are willing to partake in dirty sexting, you can make this work!

However, if you have a bf/gf in another city/state – you CANNOT turn into that person who doesn't go out anymore because they'd rather stay home and talk to their significant other on the phone. You can't stop having fun because you're always waiting to talk to them and wondering what they're up to. You can't stop hanging out with your friends because "you see no point in going out if you aren't out to meet a guy/girl."

As well, all relationships (and especially LDRs) are bidirectional. You can't expect your other half to ALWAYS visit you. You have to share the traveling. Not only can it get pricey, but it's just not fair.

This also holds true for "short term LDRs" – meaning those LDRs that are just for a period of time, i.e., a boyfriend on a med school rotation in another city for six weeks, girlfriend finishing law school, etc.

So, are LDRs impossible? No, not at all. Many turn out to be very successful! However, they do require work on both ends. It's not easy to be away from your significant other for an extended period of time.

And, I will repeat, you've got to keep the momentum up in terms of the sex life if you plan to partake in an LDR. Phone sex, Skype sex, sexting, sending pictures, WHATEVER…you have got to do to keep it going.

For those currently in an LDR, I wish you luck! And for those debating one, I think it's quite possible to do so successfully.

Only time (and distance) will tell.

The meeting of the parents...

What to wear, how to act, what to say, what not to say, and when to partake in said activity? Look no further, dear readers; I'm here to help!

Where to begin – let's start with WHEN is the right time to meet the parents.

It all depends on a few things.

If your parents don't live in the same city where you and your significant other reside, it may not be so often your parents are in town. If they come in once every six months, you may want to jump on the "meeting the parents"' bandwagon when the opportunity arises.

For example, my ex-boyfriend and I lived in (insert name of city here), but his parents lived elsewhere. We had only been dating two months at the time, but his parents happened to be in town, which didn't happen so often. Long story short, I met them that weekend, only two months in.

I feel these days, though, the meeting of the parents isn't as huge of a deal as it once was (back when our parents were in their 20s.) No, I don't mean that your bang buddy should be meeting your parents although, my good friend once had a bang buddy sleep over and his parents happened to be in town and at his apartment the next morning, so this lovely girl got to do the stride of pride right past his parents...good times. But, if it's someone you've been exclusively dating for a few months, the meeting of the parents seems quite normal!

OK, so if your parents don't live where you live, and they happen to be in town one weekend, and you happen to have been dating someone for a few months, introducing both parties is not a bad idea!

If your parents live in the same place that you and your significant other live in, there's not such a rush. This can happen really at any time.

Ladies, please let the men take the lead on this one. There's nothing that scares a guy more than a girl initiating the meeting of the parents. Guys are scared of future, marriage, commitment, and the last thing that will help these situations is: "Baby, my parents really want to meet you – how about I set up a dinner next week?" BAD, BAD, BAD. Don't do that, girls!!! Let HIM initiate. EVEN if your parents don't live in the same city as you, sweet girl, and they are in town one weekend – let him say, "Oh, I'd love to meet them if that's OK with you." This is NOT something you take the lead on. Never ever.

One story I must add in because it is nothing short of hilarious…the surprise attack. Ladies, NEVER EVER EVER do this!! My male friend was hanging out at his friend's apartment, and a girl he was hooking up with told him to come to a bar nearby. He figured it was for drinks and then he'd be having sex in no time. Little did he know, she was with HER PARENTS. He was clearly feeling uncomfortable, so she left with him to go back to his apartment. So, not only did the surprise of meeting her parents happen, but now the parents were well aware that he was about to take their precious daughter back to his apartment and bang her.

NEVER SURPRISE YOUR GUY WITH THE MEETING OF THE PARENTS. And, if you're wondering, he most certainly never saw this girl again.

However, boys, even though you're the perpetrator for this activity, I wouldn't offer your parents on a silver platter two weeks into a relationship. THAT could (and would) scare most girls.

All right, onto what to wear to meet the parents…

This shouldn't be too difficult. Maybe we should start with what NOT to wear.

Ladies – you are NOT allowed to wear anything short, revealing, tight, low cut, or, for lack of a better word, SLUTTY. No, this does not mean you need to wear a long sleeve turtleneck, pants, and a ski jacket. You just can't look like you're going to the club.

Think blazers, modest dresses, casual tops with jeans. Guys – think button down or polo shirt (depending on the time of day) with jeans and depending on where you're going, a blazer could work, too. No vintage worn in tees. (As much as I love those, maybe not the best idea for meeting the parents.)

Now that we have the *when to meet* and *what to wear* down, we can discuss how to act/what to say and not say!

You, of course, want to make a good impression on the parents of your significant other. After all, these could be your in-laws one day. (Ha ha ha, I'm kidding here. Let's not jump the gun.) Regardless, you want them to like you and you want them to give good feedback to their son or daughter.

Don't try to be someone you're not. If your significant other's parents are in a field you know nothing about, don't pretend you do. You will just look dumb! Act natural and be yourself. They will see right through you if you're not.

Don't talk too much or too fast. We all know people have a tendency to ramble (and talk fast) when they're nervous. Don't do this. It's just annoying. Carry on a conversation, but make sure they are able to get a word in!

Ask questions, be engaging, answer their questions, look them in the eye when speaking to them, smile, be pleasant, and DON'T be nervous. This is NOT the biggest deal. No need for nerves. If their son or daughter is crazy about you—which, at this point, I'd like to think they are, if you're meeting the parents—there is nothing to worry about!

It's possible the parents may be VERY different from you and your own parents in every regard. You just got to go with it. Make it work. Smile, talk, and at least pretend you're enjoying yourself.

In terms of alcohol, LET THE PARENTS (or your significant other) TAKE THE LEAD ON THIS. The parents may not drink at all (and you may drink A LOT.) You cannot be the first to order an alcoholic beverage. If you are asked for your drink order first, order water or some other non-alcoholic beverage. If your bf/gf orders a cocktail or wine or the parents do, then feel free.

And, finally, if you're going to your significant other's house to meet the parents for the first time, you must bring something. DO NOT go overboard (that looks silly), but something is certainly necessary. If you'll be eating a meal with them, some sort of dessert always works.

You can never go wrong with flowers, either. This is a first meeting – you should stick to something in the food category or flowers, but you must bring something. It's a nice gesture, and the parents will absolutely appreciate it.

The meeting will be over before you know it! Just RELAX.

Whatever you do, DO NOT talk about milking your cat. Please leave that to Gaylord Focker.

GOOD LUCK!

Is it really just a number?

You know you've all been there. That dreaded moment where your significant other asks you how many people you've slept with. If you're a guy and you've slept with very few, you're embarrassed. If you're a guy and you've slept with more than you'd like to admit, you think she'll judge and think you're a player. If you're a girl and you've slept with very few, you think you may look too innocent, but if you're a girl and you've slept with way too many, you don't want to be coined as a "slut." However, you don't want to lie. What do you do?!

I feel the "number" conversation isn't THAT big of a deal. I mean, NO, I don't think your number needs to be broadcasted on CNN, but I feel if it comes up, it's not the end of the world. I, personally, don't feel how many girls my guy has slept with defines who he is. I honestly don't care about my man's past, as long as it's over and done with. Do I LOVE the idea that my man might have slept with thirty girls before me? No, of course not, but it's water under the bridge. If I'm dating a guy who I'm crazy about, it's not the end of the world if I'm lucky number 31.

I understand that a guy may not want to share his number if I'm only the third girl he's slept with, BUT there may be reasons for this. Maybe he was in back to back serious relationships for years, so he didn't have the chance to "sleep around." Fair enough. I will say if the reason is just that he doesn't like sex, and that's why his number is so low, well that's a MAJOR problem, and we can get into that later.

If the guy doesn't want to share his number because it's so high – again, who cares? You have a past. I have a past. We all have pasts. I don't really care if you slept with every sorority girl on campus. That was five years ago! As long as you're not currently sleeping with every girl who lives in Murray Hill, we're good to go.

As for the girl – if you've slept with more guys than you'd like to admit, and it's something you keep to yourself always, then that's fine! You don't need to lie and say you slept with three guys when it's really 33, but you can give an over/under. One day down the road, after you've been dating for a longer period of time, you can admit it. I promise he won't break up with you because of this. It's in the PAST.

If you're a girl and have slept with no one, well, first, you NEED to get on that. You're missing out on one of the greatest pleasures in life. You CANNOT lie about that and if you do, he will figure it out in NO time. The guy NEEDS to know he's about to take your v card. And, boys, good luck to you there.

If you've slept with a very small number of men, that's not bad! A guy will likely prefer the idea that you weren't banging every boy in Sig Nu back in college. Don't be ashamed that you've only had sex with three guys.

Ultimately, I don't think this is an important conversation to have. If it does come up, I just don't think it's a big deal either. Lying will get you nowhere and end up leaving you and your significant other in a fight. Share your number (or play the over/under game), and move on. It's in the past. If you're going to let the past dictate your current relationship, you need to rethink things.

BUT that's just me.

At the end of the day, it's up to you to determine how your significant other will feel about this conversation. If you know it is going to cause a major fight, then don't bring it up! If it happens to come up for whatever reason, deal with it, don't lie, and don't freak out; just deal with it.

And, for those of you who actually don't know your number or don't want to admit you have a list somewhere in your room, on your iPad, or in your planner, then better for you! You just have to guesstimate and work backwards from that after prom party circa 2008.

1, 2, 3, 4, 5, 6, 7……

Slumber Party Time!

There comes a point in every (err – almost every) relationship where you start having the infamous sleepover with your significant other. This is an exciting time. Falling asleep next to your current heartthrob, waking up next to that special person, and of course, lots of sexy time in between the sheets. It's a bit of a turning point in your relationship, especially when the sleepovers start happening on a more frequent basis. Sometimes it almost becomes routine and assumed. *Your place or mine tonight*?

What tends to be a question in many relationships (at least at the beginning) is how much is too much, in terms of the boyfriend/girlfriend sleepover? What starts out to happen once to twice or three times a week turns into almost nightly, week after week. Is this OK? Is this detrimental to the relationship? Is this just too much?

There is no "rule" for this. It's up to the couple to decide what works best for them, and by them we mean BOTH of you – meaning you're in agreement, ok? However, if one or both of you start becoming far too lazy—in terms of seeing your friends, going out, ever leaving the couch—start taking some nights off from each other so you can SEE your friends, GO out, and LEAVE the couch. It's healthy, I promise!!

I know, I get it – it's so easy (AND FUN) to have sleepovers all the time. But if you're not engaged or married, you need to leave a little room for "missing each other" or wondering what the other person is up to. Making it so easy and accessible is unnecessary in the early stages of a relationship. You both had lives before you entered each other's; don't give those up now that you're an item.

This is not to say you need to have a set weekly sleepover schedule with your significant other (seems a bit rigid, if you ask me), but be cautious of the beginning of a relationship and the quantity of sleepovers.

Ideal scenario, I believe, after having been through the slumber party ring around, is weekends and just a couple nights during the week. Of course, there are exceptions if you're out of town one weekend or are crazy with work. Who knows? But, at the beginning there's no need to spend every waking minute together. Once you start doing that, and losing your "single" self, it's hard to get it back, and it's easy to become super dependent on your significant other.

Nights off are good!! I, personally, had a hard time understanding that, at first, in a serious relationship way back. Since we once went two weeks straight with back to back sleepovers (towards the beginning of our relationship), it became routine in my mind, so when he finally brought up the idea of taking nights off here and there, I took it the wrong way, and it turned into a minor disagreement. (Oops – you live, you learn.)

You have your whole life to be engaged/married, live together, and play house. Keep a bit of your worlds separate for now! It's a smart thing to do.

Canoodle away and sweet dreams.

The chameleon dater

I'll admit, off the bat, I've been guilty of, at times, falling into the chameleon dater category. (Hey, at least I 'm honest)!

What is a chameleon dater, you ask?

It is when, like a chameleon, you blend in with your surroundings…in this case, with your boyfriend's world.

For example, your boyfriend is obsessed with the Yankees, and I mean could be one of their top 10 fans EVER, so you start to follow and LOVE the Yankees. Yes, this happened to me. My high school boyfriend was a die-hard fan, didn't miss watching (or going to) a game, knew every fact about every player that ever existed, and when we started dating, I joined him in watching (or going to) games. I started obsessively following them, and I was now their #11th biggest fan!

So, is this a bad thing?

No, not necessarily. It's only natural that you start doing activities together and enjoying certain pastimes together since you are now in a relationship.

You happen to be over at your boyfriend's apartment and he only listens to Phish. Well, it's normal that you're going to start knowing Phish, appreciating Phish, and maybe start listening to Phish on your own.

The problem comes when you start doing something your boyfriend loves to do (or listening to/watching something your boyfriend loves to listen to/watch) even when you DON'T honestly enjoy it. It's one thing to do so when you're together, but when you're alone in your apartment don't start forcing yourself to enjoy watching *Family Guy* if you genuinely hate *Family Guy*. That's just not natural, fun, or really attractive. (Guys like girls who have an opinion and also who have their own passions.)

It's great that your significant other is opening you up to a new world of options. Never thought you'd be into jazz? Your boyfriend loves jazz and takes you to a few concerts and now you really appreciate it and enjoy listening to it. That's great! But only if you genuinely enjoy it.

When you're dating someone, your worlds are supposed to collide. That's what happens in relationships. It's fun and exciting and how it should be.

Just make sure you always stay true to yourself and you don't lose yourself in this person. You should still have your own passions and interests. You are who you are and shouldn't be expected to change for anyone. (Man, that's cliché.) You love reading fashion magazines. Your boyfriend doesn't get the fashion world and sometimes even mocks it. Well, that's his problem. He can read his magazine of choice while you read yours, and there you have it. Break out a bottle of bubbly, and that sounds like a good night-in to me.

As long as you don't give up the things you love, there is NOTHING wrong with immersing yourself into his world… one hobby or genre of music or activity at a time.

He'll appreciate that you want to learn about and enjoy what he loves and enjoys.

Fair enough?

I think so.

I will say you should probably try to stick to the "good" habits of your significant others. If your boyfriend goes in and out of periods of time where he smokes cigarettes, for example, you don't necessarily NEED to follow suit. Yes, it can be rather hot to have your sexy time with him and then share a cigarette after like they do in the movies. Fine, I get that, but I would say that's one thing you don't NEED to start enjoying.

So, if there's a sea of people wearing all black—hello, midtown Manhattan—and you like to blend in, by all means – go right ahead. Nothing wrong with that. From time to time, though, it's nice to stick out, wear shocking pink and do your own thing that makes you truly happy.

Can fighting be a good thing?

I know all of you want to jump to "NO," but not so fast.

Think about it.

When two people in a relationship fight, it's usually because they spend a lot of time together, know each other very well, and they know what the other person loves, hates, and everything in between. These are all good things.

When two people in a relationship NEVER fight or bicker, you have to wonder why.

I know, I know. There are relationships out there you know of where they never fight EVER (or so they say.) For starters, you do not know what goes on behind closed doors and secondly, why aren't they bickering? Do neither of them have a voice or an opinion? Are they so similar that they agree on EVERYTHING? It's unlikely (and that just wouldn't be good, people.)

Without fighting or bickering—and no, I'm not talking about blowouts similar to the WWE, I'm more talking about differing opinions and the like—a very superficial relationship can result.

Now, those of you out there reading this that are currently in a relationship where you NEVER fight, don't get all huffy and puffy on me. I'm not saying this is the case for ALL relationships, but I am saying that bickering can be healthy. Really!

There is a difference between fighting, going to sleep angry, being stubborn and voicing your opinion, figuring out the "issue," and working to resolve it. Those are two very different things.

I've been in relationships where the fights were brutal. I've also been in relationships where we'd have differing opinions on a matter, talk through it, figure it out, and it's put behind us… after a-mazing makeup sex, of course.

I'm all about the communication factor, and I loathe going to sleep angry (whether it be with a boyfriend, a parent, a sibling, you name it.) Bickering here and there is totally fine. Totally normal. Totally acceptable. It is almost abnormal to never bicker with your significant other.

If you are one (guys or girls) who always steps down when a "fight" is starting to boil, don't step down. Do not be a pushover. Don't just say, "You're right. Let's move on." That is no way to have a relationship. Speak up. Don't yell; that's ineffective. Express how you feel, talk about the matter at hand, and put it to rest. Easy enough!

In conclusion, fighting can be a very good thing. It really can be! Through fighting you can learn a lot about your significant other and it can even bring you closer.

Next time you have a fight with your boyfriend or girlfriend, don't freak out and think it's such a bad thing.

As long as there's no smack-down (unless it's in a sexual manner), you're golden.

Zip the lips

Ladies, there are times when hinting to something may be effective and funny, but there are times when that is not the case. A time when you should not hint to something would be when it involves moving in with your boyfriend or getting engaged. Men like being in control of both these decisions, as they should be!!!

If there is a restaurant in the city you've been dying to try for "date night," casually mentioning it in conversation with your significant other or "accidentally" leaving the restaurant's business card on your boyfriend's laptop is fine to do. What is NOT fine to do is leaving a print-out on his desk from *Street Easy* of an adorable one bedroom apartment in the West Village you think would be just fabulous for the two of you.

Leaving a website up on your boyfriend's computer from the destination you want to go on the vacation you guys have been discussing – FINE.

Leaving the Tiffany's diamond ring landing page open on your man's computer – NOT FINE.

You get what I'm saying, I hope.

Men are the ones who want to decide when the moving in situation is acceptable. I know some of you out there may be feminists to a degree, but this is one case where the man really needs to take charge. You happen to mention how living together could be so much fun; well, you may think this is a casual remark that means nothing, but this may (and will) scare him. The relationship is going at the speed you've both been comfortable with. By you mentioning this huge step, it will freak him out, and he will likely start acting different. It's not because he isn't very much into you, but he's not ready for that next step, and he doesn't need to be just yet. Moving in together is a HUGE commitment, and usually the next step after that is engagement, all scary thoughts to a man.

Which leads me to the engagement talk –

UNDER NO CIRCUMSTANCES may you, sweet girl, mention anything hinting to getting engaged. There is nothing that scares a man more than this discussion. If it's a discussion that is going to come up, LET YOUR MAN TAKE THE REIGNS ON THIS. I don't care if all your friends are getting engaged; you need to wait your turn. You need to relax and enjoy your relationship as it is. Your turn will come; I promise it will. Rushing your turn will only make things worse with your boyfriend and rather than pushing you forward in your relationship, it'll take you many steps back.

Why would you want that?

Exactly. I didn't think so.

If you must, feel free to watch *Father of the Bride* or *The Proposal* as many times as you wish in the privacy of your own apartment, but do not start doing so at your boyfriend's place!!

If you must, feel free to know every single detail about engagement rings, but do not repeat these facts to your boyfriend.

If you must, feel free to browse the NY Times real estate section for apartments for your significant other and you to move into. (This is crazy, though, so please don't.) But, do not do so in the presence of your man.

Do we understand each other?

Your man is in the driver's seat for these topics, so you need to sit back, relax, and just enjoy the scenery until 'Destination: Next Big Steps' comes your way.

Public Display of Nausea

Now, don't get me wrong – kisses are great here and there from your man or woman while on the street, and I'm a big fan of the hand hold, BUT there's a line that needs to be drawn (in a permanent black felt tip pen) beyond that.

I get it – you're in love, you're happy, that's GREAT, but I'm not sure everyone else needs to see you slobbering all over each other's faces every two minutes. I mean, really; GET A ROOM.

Like I said, PDA (to a degree) is totally fine. In fact, I think it's quite necessary! You're walking down the street or out at a bar, a few pecks here and there are a-okay! Holding hands, touching each other here and there, all perfectly fine! Sucking face, not coming up for air, groping each other, practically dry humping in the street, all NOT ok.

It's just not classy, people. No one wants to see you practically having sex on the streets of New York. Really – no one does. It makes others around you feel uncomfortable. Save that for the bedroom.

I'm all about the bedroom craziness – just NOT in public. Even when you're drunk and horny, SAVE IT.

You're doing all of us a favor by keeping it G-rated in public.

I truly believe Ludacris said it best –

Lady in the street, but a freak in the bed...

Toothbrush = LOVE

The leaving of things at the significant other's apartment –

Dun dun dun.

There comes a time in every relationship when the girl "mistakenly" leaves some personal items at her boyfriend's apartment. (*Oops! Totally didn't mean to leave that there, but now that it is there, might-as-well not deal with bringing it home.*) Or...when the boyfriend gives her a spare toothbrush. (*Oh boy! he could be the one.*) This is considered a big deal to some people, and in some cases, it is.

You don't live together (yet), but you're starting to leave some things at each other's pad. These things can range from deodorant to a flat iron to shoes to boxers to face soap, and everything in between.

When is the right time to start doing this?

Depending on who you ask, you can get some VERY different answers.

Some people think it's absolutely unnecessary to leave anything at your bf/gf's apartment. They think if you're not living together, why would you do that? No need to jump the gun.

Others think at least six months should go by before doing so.

Some jump right in after only a couple short months.

Of course, it's all dependent on the two individual people and how serious/fast-moving their relationship is.

Ladies, I advise you to NOT initiate the leaving of the things at the man's apartment. This is something he should bring up. It may be annoying, but if you have to bring your makeup each time you sleep over, I'm sorry but you have to do it. Do not ask for a drawer or part of his bathroom cabinet. NO, NO, NO. This will scare him off. Let him take the reign on this one. Let him mention leaving things at his place, so you don't have to bring a whole bag every single time. Let him offer up a spare toothbrush. Let HIM initiate this. There are times you can initiate things, but this is not one of them. If he starts leaving things at your place, then you're allowed to reciprocate, but this should be on his terms.

Gentlemen, if this is something you're fully uncomfortable with, that is fine and no one is forcing you to allow your gf to leave things at your place. However, if this is not something that scares you, then you should casually mention to your lady that she should totally leave an extra deodorant or face soap or some make up or extra undergarments at your pad. Not only will it make her realize that you see this relationship lasting for more than the immediate future, but it makes it easier on her (no more lugging of the overnight bag around), and it brings you a bit closer. No need to give her half your closet, two drawers, and the medicine cabinet, but telling her she should leave a few things here and there is a nice thing to do, and no I'm not saying you should do this within the first couple months. No rush, my friend, no rush.

If you're at a place in your relationship where this comes up, good for you! And if you're not, don't start worrying, ladies. This doesn't necessarily mean ANYTHING, so don't start freaking out and picking fights with your bf about how you don't think he's serious about you because he won't let you leave your crap at his bachelor pad. Remember, pick your battles, and this should not be one of them.

Just do not start "by accident" leaving an outfit there from the night before because you happened to do the stride of pride in his big t-shirt and gym shorts the next morning. One step at a time.

REMEMBER, just because you sleep there 4-5 nights a week does not mean you live there. Let's not rush to next year, my friends.

Slow and steady wins the race….

Chapter 6

THE (E)X FILES.

Oh boy. This topic could take up an entire book for me. I've dated a decent number of guys, which means I've also been through a decent number of breakups. Some went phenomenally well and I'm still friendly with them to this day. Others I wouldn't say went phenomenally well, and we no longer speak, but we also have no hard feelings towards one another. And others were pretty much hell. No, I'm not being dramatic – it was THAT bad. All that being said, ex-partners can be a funny thing. A lot of times when people go through break ups, it doesn't just end, and it's not just a clean break. They continue to see each other, or speak, or hook up. While I don't think any of that is wise so soon after an ending, most of my friends have done something similar.

Sex with an ex – is it really ever JUST sex with an ex?

We've all been there. We've all dated someone, had mind blowing sex with them numerous times, broke up, and weeks later we're back in bed with the ex, but this time it's supposed to be just sex, the no-feelings-involved sex. HA. How often does THAT happen?

You dated this person, you may have been close to being in

love with this person, now this person is no longer in your life in that way, but you're sleeping with them, and trying so so hard to not feel, to not care, to walk out of there the next morning feeling great, fulfilled, and happy. And unfortunately, one of you feels sad, still fulfilled—I mean it was great sex, of course. You should feel fulfilled on SOME level—but now are missing your ex.

Sex with an ex is definitely exciting. It reminds you of the fun you used to have. You feel like you don't have to worry about awkwardness because you have already slept with each other so many times before. If anything, it is fun because you can be uninhibited again. The downside is obvious that you probably have a little bit of feelings for that person deep down which may or may not resurface after having sex. If that person is just in it for sex and you have feelings, you are screwed and will be worse off than before. There is a reason it is an "ex" because somebody or both checked out of the relationship for better options. If they are coming back to you, either they want you back or are just using you for sex because they are desperate and you are a safe bet. (They do not have feelings for you.) In summary, having sex with an ex should be a last resort and only if you are the one that has no feelings for the other person.

You're only hurting yourself. This typically happens for girls—but, hey, guys have feelings too…well, sometimes—but having sex with an ex will give you a false sense of hope! *(If we have sex, I know it will make him remember the good times and then he'll want to get back together with me. How could he not?)* UH, Hello, Ms. Delusional.

You will go into it sure of yourself, confident, and knowing you're about to have fantastic sex. You are likely lying to yourself if you say, "I don't have feelings for him – it's JUST sex. Really – I can handle it!" You will force yourself to think this way, but deep down you know it's not true. You will then revert back to missing this person, while he just had sex (no strings attached sex) with his ex and is probably taking a new girl out that very next night.

(And for you boys, or whomever is the one who truly has NO feelings for the other person – you will have to deal with them trying to get back together, trying to talk to you into working it out, having long elaborate conversations on the matter, etc. You may be OK with this because you REALLY just want to bang him/her no matter what, but just be cautious.)

Unless you are 150% over your ex, DO NOT (and I repeat DO NOT) have sex with them unless you are both aware of the repercussions.

And need I mention the post sex discomfort. *Guy: Shit, I really am not in the mood to cuddle and if I do, I'm giving her the wrong impression. I kind of just want her to leave. Girl: Why isn't he cuddling with me? Oh wait, I think he's about to. (Two minutes pass.) Yes, he spooned me. I knew he still had feelings for me. It feels like old times. Guy: I pray she knows I'm just doing this to be nice. I don't want to get back together with her. I really just wanted to have sex with her because while the relationship wasn't going to work, the sex was f-ing good. Damn it.*

....and so on and so forth.

Understood that it is some of the best sex you've ever had, but can't you just go find someone new to have sex with? Your ex isn't the only person who is good in bed. I know I've promised you a lot, thus far, but again, I PROMISE you it's only going to cause unnecessary drama. Who needs that?!

Conclusion: sex with an ex – not so sexy.

RUN-INS – why is the city so damn small?

I was going on a Sunday afternoon stroll with my friend years back. We did some brunching, some shopping, and some people watching. All in all it was starting off to be a great day.

All of a sudden, we're down around Union Square, my friend

grabs my hand and says under her breath, "Shit! (insert ex's name here) is right there."

Let me preface the rest of this by saying my friend and her ex had anything but a good breakup. It was messy and horrible and to this day they still aren't on the best of terms. (And, yes, it's been over two years.)

Well, at this point, he likely already saw us, so we can't run the other way. So, I told her to say, "Hi," and she did just that.

She handled it just fine – appearing calm, cool, and collected. He, on the other hand, not only looked like he just woke up, but he appeared awkward, aggravated, and annoyed because he just ran into his ex while looking the way he did.

New York City, along with many other cities out there, is just too damn small. I can't tell you how many weekends in a row I would bump into someone I knew from a "past" life at a bar. (Sometimes it's nice seeing them, and sometimes I would have rather NOT bumped into them.) It's like of ALL the bars on the lovely island of Manhattan; you just HAD to be at the one I decided to go to with all my friends tonight. UGH.

How to handle the run-in:

For starters, I know your mom may tell you this all the time and sometimes you ignore it, but really, try not to leave your apartment looking in a way you'd HATE for anyone to see you. I'm not saying you should be dressed up in your ball gown and suit and tie every time you step foot out of your building, but try to put yourself together on some level. And NO, this does not mean to deck yourself out in tons of makeup, girls, each time. That is just fake and silly especially when you're only going to the grocery store and running some errands. I just mean to look presentable. You NEVER know whom you'll meet or whom you may run into.

DO NOT run the other way once you notice this person. They will have likely already seen you, and it will look quite silly if you do such a thing.

Always appear calm and at ease when you see this person. Even if you are freaking out and having a panic attack deep down, you cannot appear that way. Wear sunglasses if out during the day, so you can cover the "shock," "anger" or "sadness" in your eyes, but please, no stunna shades at night. You are not Jay-Z!

Don't be rude and obnoxious because that's immature and pointless. Simply say, "Hello," and ask how they're doing, answer them if they ask you a question, and say, "Okay, I really need to get going – bye." (Don't say it was great to see them unless it was actually GREAT to see them.)

DO NOT squeeze your friend's arm the second you say goodbye or start screaming or freaking out. Wait until you're at least two blocks away (or at the other end of the bar) from this person and then do all the freaking out you need.

And after the run-in, run to the nearest bar and get yourself a big cocktail.

Remaining friends with your best friend's ex – yay or nay?

One may immediately want to jump to "nay" when looking at this topic, but are there ever exceptions? Is it ever okay for you to remain friendly with your friend's ex? Where does the line need to be drawn?

It all depends. On a few things.

First, is your friend okay with you being friends with the ex? If the answer to this question is "no," then look no further. There is absolutely no exception in this case. If your friend isn't comfortable with it, you cannot (under no circumstances) be friends with the ex.

If your friend hasn't really expressed a concern, please think about the following.

Did your friend and the ex have a horrendous break up and are they on not such amazing terms? If this is the case, you should not be in touch with the ex. If you happen to see them out, it's one thing, but to reach out to them for plans is unnecessary. Try to keep conversation to a minimum.

Did your friend and the ex have a decent break up and now are on fine terms? In this case, it seems okay to be friends (especially if you were close during the relationship.) Best friends? No. This is not necessary. Acquaintances? Fine. Plans every once in a rare while? Fine.

Now, if you and your friend's ex were friends prior to them dating, this is a different story. There's no reason you need to stop being friends if you have a history. You just need to be cautious. You are friends with both parties, and you don't want to lose one of them because of this situation. Be careful what you say to both people. Do not take sides. Do not gossip back and forth between one another.

However, if you and your friend's ex became best friends WHILE they were dating (meaning you met THROUGH them), this is not enough of a reason to stay friends with them if your friend says she is not 100% comfortable with it. Your loyalty lies with your friend. Yes, it's unfortunate you can't keep up the friendship with the ex, but you'll need to get over that. Your friend comes first. I'm sure you have PLENTY of other friends. No need for this one, the ex. And they will understand.

There are instances, depending on how the breakup went down, where your friend's ex will try to stay close with you solely because they want to have ties, on some level, to your friend (the ex-boyfriend/girlfriend.) By being in touch with you, it will give them a false sense of hope. It will make it harder for them to move on. If you notice this is happening, I'd cut off ties for now (for your friend's sake and for the both of them.) Maybe down the road a friendship could resurface, but soon after the breakup is just not necessary.

It's a tricky situation, but you have to be sensitive to your friends. They come first. Depending on how they feel on the matter and what terms they're on with the ex, you can then figure out if it makes sense to remain friends.

And under no circumstances can you hook up with the ex of your friend!! Just don't go there.

And no, being wasted is never an excuse. I don't care how inebriated you are, how horny you may be, how secretly attracted you've been to your friend's ex for quite some time, you cannot go down that road.

Capiche?

They call it a "break up" for a reason

I know it may be hard for some of you to realize – but a break up means just that – you're broken up. You are not together. You are not dating anymore. You aren't going to speak daily anymore. You aren't going to "flirt" back and forth on each other's Facebook walls. You aren't going to talk on gchat all day during the work day. You aren't going to sext anymore. You aren't going to go on dates together anymore. You are no longer going to have sleepovers almost nightly. You are BROKEN up. Don't mean to be harsh, but it seems some people need that kick in the butt.

Every single one of my friends has been through some sort of break up (and sometimes more than once.) Many handle it just fine, don't dwell, move on, and start hooking up, having sex, or dating someone new almost instantly. (If that's you, go you!) Some, however, have a hard time understanding what a break up means.

I've seen it all. I've seen and been through the smoothest of break ups and I've seen breakups that sort of resemble a category 5 hurricane, an F 5 tornado, and a magnitude 10 earthquake all clashing together. (And yes, I'm also one of the lucky ones who have gotten to experience that version of a breakup.)

Way back, I was talking to my friend who was going through a break up. Because I've been through the worst break up a human being could imagine, and no, I'm not exaggerating, I am now very harsh on my friends when they are about to break up with their bf, when their bf is about to break up with them, and/or when they are dealing with the aftermath. I feel I have every right to be!

When you and your significant other break up, it's DONE. You're breaking up for a reason. It's not like one or both of you just decided on that random Tuesday night that hey, *I'm just going to break up with (insert name here) for shits and giggles.* A lot of thought goes into a break up.

Because of x, y, and z reasons for this break up, it's just not going to work out right now. It's not to say it may never work again between the two of you. No one can predict the future and NO, not even the psychics on 14th street can, but at this moment in time, you are breaking up. You are leaving each other's lives.

I get it. You've been dating for two years. You've done so much together. You know each other's families. You've spent most nights together. You're best friends with each other's friends. You have vacationed together. You have spoken about moving in together down the road. You have a life of your own, but this other person had a major place in it. You had a routine together. I get it.

Great.

But now it's done.

So, move on.

Yes, we know. It's easier said than done. I know. I know.

If you choose not to move on, that's fine (and your loss), but at least stop dwelling day in and day out on your relationship that just ended. You are allowed a few days or weeks of "grieving," crying, and venting to friends. Of course you are. It's necessary. After that period of time though, don't give your ex so much credit. Don't let him/her have that much power over you and your feelings!!

I understand it may take a while to be 100% over your ex and what you shared. (Fine, that's understandable; it was a serious relationship.) But, you've got to at least attempt to move on, stop thinking about him/her, stop thinking about what could have been, stop beating yourself up over what you could have done differently, and stop analyzing everything. LET. IT. GO.

If you want the chance to even consider getting back together, you've got to sever ties completely for at least a little while. No, I don't mean days. I mean weeks, maybe months. You need to actually let the breakup BE for a while.

If it's just too hard for you to accept this, and you want to still talk, and this that and the other – that's not really a break up. In fact, it won't allow either of you to move on. If your ex needs space and asks you to respect his/her wishes of not being in touch and not seeing each other, you really have no choice. You need to respect those wishes. And really – you have NO choice.

Trust me, if you don't listen it will only push them further and further and further and further and further away.

If you want to even attempt a friendship, well for starters that may or may not be wise, but if it's even a remote possibility, you have got to give it a rest for a while. It's not happening overnight.

I will reiterate – when you break up, you're BREAKING UP. You're no longer together. Stay away from delusional thoughts because it will only make it harder. Move on, go find a sexy rebound, keep yourself busy, start dating, and let it go.

Some DOs and DONTs when dealing with a breakup:

- DO vent and cry to your friends for a few days, if needed.
- DO flirt with that hot guy or girl you always see at the gym (or on the subway, or really anywhere.)
- DO have no strings attached sex. (Well, only if you

can handle it, and you don't start crying while doing the deed because of thoughts of your ex.)

- DO keep yourself busy.
- DO live up the single life. (It can be really VERY fun.)
- DO enjoy "ME" time.
- DON'T dwell and look at old pictures of you and your ex when you were both happy together because that's a waste of your time, and you'll probably start crying alone in your apartment and that's just not OK or cool on any level.
- DON'T call incessantly in the hopes this will change the ex's mind on the break up because they won't, and you bugging them isn't going to be the reason for any change.
- DON'T reach out to your ex's friends – those people are his/her territory – not yours.
- DON'T look all over Facebook to see what they are up to because, yes, they may have met someone else, and it's not necessary for you to see that.
- DON'T talk about your ex on dates – couldn't be further from attractive.
- DON'T think your life is over because it's not, and it's slightly dramatic for you to think such silly thoughts. Stop being sad and start living again. Honestly.

Sorry to be harsh, but I think it is necessary.
I still love you all.

Your ex's friends

Let's talk about your EX's friends. Let me repeat, your EX's friends, not YOUR friends.

Now, when you're dating someone, you start hanging out with their friends a lot, and naturally, you become close with some of those friends. That's fine and great. You're in with the friends – good job!

The problem arises when the breakup occurs. These were your ex's friends to begin with. Their loyalty lies with him/her, and they sometimes just need to cut you off because it's not fair to your ex. Unless you have a very amicable break up (which, rumor has it, is possible), you should not be in contact with your ex's friends…at all.

It's one thing if they reach out to you for some reason or another, but in most instances, you and your ex's friends should not be friends.

I get that it may seem unnatural to just stop talking to someone with no explanation, but in this case you just need to move on, understand that it's nothing against you, and let it go. These are your ex's friends – not yours. While they became your good friends during your relationship, if it weren't for your ex, you likely would never have met them.

You had enough friends and a full life PRIOR to your relationship, so there is no reason you are in desperate need of their friends POST relationship.

If you see them out, it's one thing, but to go out of your way to make plans with them or constantly speak to them, that is just not right. And you're probably just going to piss your ex off if you try to remain buddy buddy with these people. And you don't want that.

Down the road maybe it's possible to reconnect, but soon after the breakup and for the many months following it – stay away from your ex's world.

It's called a break up because you're doing just that – breaking off your relationship, your lives together, and everything in between (including the friends.)

But they're so much fun!! They have the best parties, go on the best trips, and we always had the best time together.

Tough luck, kiddo.

We get it. My ex had a really awesome group of guy friends, and I was extremely upset I was losing them along with him, BUT it's what had to be. Your ex's friends are not your territory, and there are NO exceptions to that rule.

None.

Sorry to be blunt, but I've got to be because so many people seem to not understand this unwritten rule.

Well, now it's written.

Reconnecting with the ex

So, ladies and gentlemen, this is an interesting question. You date someone for a certain amount of time, you break up, a certain amount of time passes, and both have hopefully "moved on" in some form or another. Is it ever necessary to reconnect with the infamous ex?

Now, it all depends on the relationship, the breakup, and the aftermath, I feel, if it is ever a wise or necessary idea to reconnect with a past relationship.

A couple scenarios:

Let's say you and this ex dated for years on and off, but ultimately broke up because you both saw no future. It was a mutual break up, you went your separate ways, and now you're both in new relationships. I see no reason at all you can't catch up with this ex every now and then. You ended on fine terms, you dated for a long time, and you have no hard feelings regarding the relationship or the break up. Catching up every now and then is PERFECTLY fine. Of course, make sure your current bf/gf is kept apprised of the situation. Exes can always be a sticky situation, so just make sure they know there is nothing to worry about at all. And make sure you have no feelings for your ex anymore whatsoever.

Now, let's say you and this ex dated for a period of time, but ultimately feelings faded on one side for whatever the reason may be. One of you initiated the break up and the other one of you was not having it. The one who was not having it did not want to end this relationship and took it horribly. In this case, a significant period of time needs to pass before any reconnection with the ex takes place. Trust me on this one! If you reconnect too soon, the one who did not want this break up will think each "reconnection" is a chance to "win" the other person's heart back. It will give him/her a false sense of hope EACH time you see each other or talk. In this case, a significant amount of time needs to pass (and I mean significant – not just a month or two) before this takes place. And if you still have even the slightest of feelings for said ex, keep your distance.

OK, let's say you and your ex dated for a decent amount of time, and as time went on you both realized you needed time apart because something was just not there anymore, so after debating what to do, you ultimately broke up, both agreeing it was the right thing to do. While you both KNEW it was what needed to happen, one of you didn't WANT it to happen, BUT it still happened. You talked, went your separate ways, and one of you just couldn't handle being apart and you did not take it so well. (Actually, you took it horribly.) Granted, you both knew this should happen, but you didn't want to see it. One thing led to another and the aftermath of the breakup turned into a category 5 hurricane, more like a category 5 hurricane meets an F8 tornado. In this case, A LOT of time needs to pass before any reconnection could take place. Not months, more like over a year…maybe even closer to 2 years. Enough time needs to pass to make sure both people have "moved on" from the horrible resentment you built up during the aftermath, and enough time for both people to have moved on from the feelings they once had for each other. After both of these things have taken place, feel free to reconnect, if both people are willing to do so.

How about if you and your ex dated only for a few months, broke up because the spark died, and so be it? In this case, not TOO much time needs to pass before the reconnection. Make sure you're both over the short-lived relationship, but assuming this doesn't take too long, which it shouldn't because it was only a few months. Reconnecting and talking from time to time are certainly fine and harmless!

Now, you were in a relationship and one of you ends up moving to another city for work, and you break up because you don't want to deal with a long distance relationship. In this case, if both people understand the situation and agree that an LDR is not what either of you signed up for at the moment, reconnecting soon after is fine, if BOTH parties are fine with it. If only one person was anti-LDR and the other wanted to attempt it, make sure you don't stay in touch or it will give the one who wanted the LDR a false sense of hope, and that's not the fun kind of hope to have.

There are tons of scenarios I could go through, but I think you get the point. Is it ever crucial to reconnect with your ex? No, not necessarily, but is it the worst idea in the world? Again, not necessarily. It all depends on how the breakup went down, and most importantly, how much time has gone by since.

In conclusion, I am certainly not against the reconnection with the ex, but I do feel one needs to be very cautious prior to doing so. Make sure enough time has passed for both parties, make sure you have both moved on in one way or another, make sure you are in a different place than you were at the break up, and make sure you don't jump in the sack with them. Otherwise, you're good to go.

As the old saying goes – time heals all.

Tick tock tick tock…

How long is too long?

How long is too long to mourn a breakup?

I'm totally 100% guilty of dwelling on a past relationship and break up, so if I had been writing this years back, I would have been a huge hypocrite. Luckily, we are not years back, and I can totally and fully be blunt and harsh with you. Ready?

Under no circumstances am I a proponent of the long drawn out tearful mourning of the ex. Sorry, but I'm just NOT ok with it.

Understandably so, everyone needs to mourn their breakup however best suits them. Fine. I will grant you a few days, maybe even a week or two of venting to your friends, crying (directed towards girls) and doing all the typical breakup shenanigans. Fair enough.

After that allotted period of time is up, though, you need to move on. Really, you do! You are wasting precious time dwelling and thinking about someone who has broken up with you. I am going to spell it out for you. This boy or girl has broken up with you (whether you originally agreed with the idea or not) because for whatever the reason may be they do not want to be with you at this moment in time. They have made up their mind. Do not try to fight it. Who knows what the future may bring, but at this moment this person does not want to be in a relationship with you at all. I'm sorry, but they don't! Why would you want to be with someone who doesn't want to be with you?

LET. IT. GO.

You dwelling a. will hinder you from meeting another person

b. is just super unattractive and c. is the biggest waste of energy. (I mean – isn't it exhausting?!)

If this person wants to reach out to you or get back together with you, trust me, they WILL go after you no matter what. So, you sulking around and being depressed about the situation is really just silly. No one wants to be around a depressed person. Really. It makes you about 15 times less attractive, and who wants that?!

Not me!

Ladies, men compartmentalize their thoughts. It's how they are programmed. When they want to think about sports, they think about sports. When they want to think about work, they think about work. And when they want to think about breaking up, they think about it, make their decision, and that's that.

Women, on the other hand, are like a bowl of spaghetti. (My friend once made this comparison). Women have a million different thoughts in their heads at any one given time, sometimes a jumbled mess. They don't necessarily know how to turn off (or compartmentalize) those thoughts; hence, they sometimes have a long drawn out break up process. Of course, this isn't the case all the time, but you get where I am going with this.

So, this is me telling you that you are wasting such valuable time dwelling over someone who does not want to be with you right now. While there is no set time limit for one to get over their ex—because, yes, I am a sympathetic person when it comes down to it, and everyone deserves time to "mourn" this loss—I HIGHLY advise you to force yourself to move on as quickly as humanly possible.

Don't sit there looking through old Facebook photos remembering the good times you once had. Delete those photos if you have no self-restraint because the good times are no longer. Uh, hello! We are in the present day. Last time I checked the past isn't coming back, so why are you hanging out back there. Earth to you, dear reader, it's way more fun up here!

But what if he changes? What if he has already changed?! We could make this work. I know it's going to work!

Do me a favor and stop thinking these thoughts.

STOP! Do not pass go. Do not collect $200. Just stop!

So be it if he changes. That's not your problem or concern. Your problem and concern is to move yourself on, to stop dwelling, and to start living again inclusive of rebounds, dates, bang buddies, interim bang buddies, summer flings, girls' nights out, boys' nights out, wine, wine and more wine or your liquor of choice, and anything else that gets you back on your feet.

Do we understand each other?

You're nothing short of amazing, and your prince (or princess) in shining armor is out there, and you'll meet them soon enough, if not already.

In summary, life in your 20s is nothing short of epic and pretty damn fantastic. Enjoy every moment and have fun. I hope you not only found this handbook entertaining, but learned a thing or two, as well.

Julie

'OOPS' WORD LIST

Bang Buddy – (noun): Someone you have a strictly physical relationship with. ("I'm so horny; I'm going to text my **bang buddy** and see if she will come over tonight and get me out of this drought!")

Bigger Better Deal aka BBD – (noun): Not the person you're dating, but rather the person you want to be dating, and who you think might be better for you than your current interest. ("I mean I really do like (insert name here), but he's missing so many of the parts I feel like I really want in a guy/girl; I know, I'm looking for the **BBD**.")

Chameleon Dater – (noun): One who tends to pick up all the same interests and hobbies and passions as their significant other. ("Damn, she is such a **chameleon dater**. Every time she dates a new guy, she has a new favorite Pandora station or is suddenly a fan of a different sports team.")

Doorman Dating – (noun): The practice of searching for someone to date by way of the doormen in the building you live. ("**Doorman dating** is the best! My doorman set me up with someone on the 6th floor, and we totally hit it off.")

Down to F*ck aka DTF – (verb): When you are horny and in the mood to have sexual intercourse. ("I'm so **DTF** it's not even funny!!")

Define the Relationship aka DTR – (verb): The conversation that comes up regarding the status of you and the person you are seeing. ("Ugh, she wants to **DTR**, and I just want to bang.")

Group Hang – (noun): A modern way of dating where it's not just a one-on-one date, but rather a group of people hanging out on your "date." ("Last night was fun. It was a **group hang**, and all of his friends were there.")

Interim Bang Buddy – (noun): Someone you have a strictly physical relationship with for a short period of time. ("So pumped. (Insert name here) is in town for the summer, and she's totally going to be my **interim bang buddy** until (insert name here) comes back in the fall.")

Manboy – (noun): Not old enough (or mature enough) to be considered a man, but not young enough to be considered a boy. ("He's such a **manboy**, but maybe soon enough he'll graduate to the status of an actual man!")

Nooner – (noun): The act of going home during the work day for a quick hook up, i.e., sex and then going back to work afterwards. ("Down for a **nooner** today? I only have a 30 minute lunch break. Meet at my place in 20. I'll be quick.")

Sexile – (noun): The act of kicking your roommate or friend out of the room or apartment in order for you to hook up with the person you are currently seeing or having sex with. ("Dude, I hate to do this, but I have to **sexile** you. (Insert name here) is coming over in an hour, and it's going to be a noisy few hours, if you know what I mean").

Sexting – (verb): Sending text messages that are more sexual than the average text message you send. ("He's been **sexting** me all day. We're totally hooking up this weekend.")

Tonsil Hockey – (noun): An intense version of a make out session. ("Such a bummer. She came over and all we did was play **tonsil hockey** and nothing else!")

Made in the USA
Columbia, SC
31 January 2018